Osmon Cleander Baker

A Guide-Book in the Administration of the Discipline

Of the Methodist Episcopal Church

Osmon Cleander Baker

A Guide-Book in the Administration of the Discipline
Of the Methodist Episcopal Church

ISBN/EAN: 9783337162238

Printed in Europe, USA, Canada, Australia, Japan

Cover: Foto ©Lupo / pixelio.de

More available books at **www.hansebooks.com**

A GUIDE-BOOK

IN THE

ADMINISTRATION OF THE DISCIPLINE

OF THE

Methodist Episcopal Church.

BY OSMON C. BAKER, D. D.

Adapted to the Discipline of 1884.

NEW YORK:
PHILLIPS & HUNT.
CINCINNATI:
CRANSTON & STOWE.
1884.

Entered according to Act of Congress, in the year 1873, by

NELSON & PHILLIPS,

in the Office of the Librarian of Congress at Washington.

EDITORIAL NOTE.

IN this edition the principles and precedents of ecclesiastical jurisprudence, as set forth by Bishop Baker in former editions, have not been materially modified. Such changes, however, have been made as were rendered necessary by the legislation of the last General Conference, and it is believed that the work will still be found, as heretofore, an important aid to pastors in administering the Discipline of the Church.

NEW YORK, *October*, 1884.

PREFACE.

THE design of this little manual is to furnish junior preachers with a brief, plain Guide for the correct discharge of their official duties. We have made no attempt to explain and defend our ecclesiastical system; this has been sufficiently done in several popular works, which are widely spread among our people. Nor have we aimed at endeavouring to impress our rising ministry with a deeper sense of ministerial obligation, and to set forth the moral and religious elements which compose the character of "able ministers of the New Testament." There are already many extensive and able treatises upon these varied topics. But there is a demand, we apprehend, for a practical work which shall descend to the very minutiæ of the pastor's daily duties.

In preparing our manual, we have found ourselves treading in an unbeaten path: no work of this kind has been attempted, if we may except Bishop Hedding's most admirable "Discourse on the Administration of the Discipline." This discourse has created a desire for a more extended work of the same general character. By the extension and division of our work, the young preacher is now often necessarily put immediately in pastoral charge, and is consequently deprived of the counsels and experience of senior preachers, which were formerly enjoyed.

We are not unaware of the difficulty of furnishing a work which shall be generally acceptable, from the different usages which prevail, to some extent, in different parts of the country, and the conflicting opinions of leading men: but it has been our aim to ascertain the general views of the best informed upon the several topics discussed, and to present them in a brief and lucid manner.

We have endeavoured to give particular attention to the several sections relating to Church trials; guarding, on the one hand, against too close an analogy to civil proceedings and mere ecclesiastical technicalities; and, on the other, against a loose and arbitrary mode of procedure. The evils which the Church has suffered from these causes should put every administrator on his guard. But we have found it impossible to express our meaning with clearness and precision without employing legal terms more frequently than we have desired.

This work is not presented as an *official* one; it is simply suggestive and advisory, for which the author is alone responsible. It is not a record of legal decisions by which the administration of the Church is to be governed, but a brief compend, exhibiting rather the *usage* than the *law* of the Church. Most appropriately can we employ the language of our late senior bishop: "I have not the vanity to suppose it is free from errors, but it is an offering of the best light I have on the subject. It may be proper to say, however, that on most of the points which contain opinions on discipline I have conversed frequently and largely with many of our most enlightened and able ministers, and they agree with these opinions."

For many years past, we have noted down every valuable suggestion which we have heard or read relating to our practical economy; and having modified, written, and rewritten many of them frequently, we are not able now to give the credit which is due for many of these suggestions. At the earnest request of many friends this little manual is given to the public, hoping that it may prove a *vade mecum* to the young minister, and render some aid in the discharge of the duties of the pastorate.

CONTENTS.

CHAPTER I.
Church Membership.

Section I.—*Members.*

	Page
1. Pastors the constituted authority to receive members	21
2. Membership should not depend upon a vote	22
3. Receiving members residing in another charge	22
4. How expelled members can be received	23
5. How withdrawn members can be received	24
6. Reception of members from other orthodox Churches	24
7. Orthodox Churches defined	24
8. Membership when the administration has been incorrect	25

Section II.—*Probationers.*

1. Caution in receiving members on trial	26
2. By whom received	27
3. General qualifications required	27
4. Period of probation	28
5. Rights and privileges of probationers	29
6. Not liable to Church trial	29

Section III.—*Withdrawal.*

1. Church relation depends upon the pleasure of the parties	31
2. When the Church can be a party to a withdrawal	32
3. When a member can claim a right to withdraw	32
4. The Church may suffer a withdrawal	33
5. Relation of societies which reject regularly appointed pastors	34
6. When a request to withdraw can be recalled	34
7. Relation of such persons as refuse to perform their covenant vows	35
8. To whom the request to withdraw to be presented	35

CHAPTER II.

THE CONFERENCES.

SECTION I.—*Annual Conferences.*

	Page
1. First annual conference	35
2. Districts	36
3. Circuits	37
4. Relation of episcopacy to the general and annual conferences	38
5. Prerogatives of the president of an annual conference	39
6. Division of circuits	41
7. Episcopal decisions	42
8. Commencement of conference year	43
9. Special transfers	43
10. Who must attend conference	44
11. Preachers refusing to go to their work	44
12. The General Conference order about receiving members	45
13. Demanding a location	46
14. When the act of location takes place	46
15. Certificate of location	46
16. Readmission	46
17. Withdrawal a bar to readmission	46
18. Preachers from any branch of the Methodist Church, or from any Church agreeing with us in doctrines	47
19. Admission from other Churches	47
20. Rights of superannuated preachers, and their quarterly conference relations	47
21. Preacher on trial	48
22. Term of service on an individual charge	48
23. Every effective preacher must receive an appointment	48
24. Preachers appointed to schools and colleges	48
25. Preachers on trial	49
26. Advisory character of conference requests respecting appointments	49
27. Rights of transferred ministers	49

SECTION II.—*District Conferences.*

1. When district conferences may be held	50
2. Of whom composed	50

CONTENTS.

	Page
3. Meets once or twice a year	51
4. President	51
5. Powers of district conferences	51
6. Candidates must be recommended	52
7. Are not authorized to renew licenses	52
8. To inquire about collections and opportunities for labor.	53

Section III.—*Quarterly Conferences.*

1. Origin of quarterly conferences	53
2, 3. Powers	54
4. Members	55
5. President	56
6. Secretary	56
7. Power over Sunday-schools and Sunday-school societies	56
8. Sunday-school report of preacher to be journalized	57
9. Time of holding quarterly conference, how fixed	57
10. Adjourning from day to day	57
11. Adjourned by the president	57
12. Temperance	57
13. Quorum	58
14. Approval of the minutes	58

Section IV.—*Leaders and Stewards' Meetings.*

1. Origin of leaders' meetings	58
2. Of whom composed	60
3. Powers and duties	60
4. To whom class-leaders are responsible	62

CHAPTER III.

Ministers.

Section I.—*Bishops.*

1. How appointed	63
2. Duties of	63

Section II.—*Presiding Elders.*

1. Origin of the office	63
2. Nature of it	63
3. Decision of law questions	64
4. Relation to individual societies	64
5. Permitting a preacher to leave his work	65

CONTENTS.

	Page
6. Power to remove preachers................................	65
7. Limitation of time applied to superannuated and local preachers...	65
8. Superintendents of domestic missions	65
9. Testimonials of applicants for foreign missions.........	66
10. Subjects of missionary correspondence.................	67
11. Presiding in an annual conference.....................	67

Section II.—*Preacher in Charge.*

1. The term defined.....................................	68
2. Duties of the preacher in charge......................	68
3. To whom responsible..................................	72

Section III.—*Local Preachers.*

1. Mode of obtaining license.............................	73
2. By whom given	73
3. Renewal of license refused without impeachment.......	73
4. How long a license is valid............................	74
5. Ecclesiastical year defined	74
6. Ordained local preachers..............................	75
7. Recommendation to travel	75
8. To whom amenable...................................	76
9. Prerequisites for ordination...........................	76
10. When local preachers from British, Irish, and Canada conferences are eligible...........................	77
11. How long recommendations are valid..................	77
12. Control of appointments	78
13. Withdrawal of local preachers........................	78

Section IV.—*Exhorters.*

1. Early recognized	78
2. Duties of exhorters...................................	78
3. Under the direction of the preacher in charge..........	79
4. Who are eligible to be exhorters......................	79
5. By whom licensed....................................	80
6. To whom responsible....	80

CHAPTER IV.

CERTIFICATES AND LOVE-FEASTS.

SECTION I.—*Note of Recommendation.*

		Page
1.	Who are entitled to such note	81
2.	Withholding a certificate	81
3.	Who are not entitled to a certificate	81
4.	Removal without a certificate	82
5.	To whom a member is responsible after he has taken a letter	82
6.	How long a certificate remains valid	82
7.	All proper certificates to be received	83
8.	To whom certificates should not be given	84
9.	By whom certificates must be given	84
10.	Certificates to those who withdraw	85
11.	Certificate of official standing	85
12.	To notify the pastor within whose bounds the member removes	85

SECTION II.—*Love-Feasts.*

1.	Origin of love-feasts	85
2.	Why discontinued	86
3.	Design of their institution in our Church	87
4.	Love-feast tickets	88
5.	Who may be admitted	88
6.	Love-feasts at the quarterly meeting	88

CHAPTER V.

CHURCH TRIALS.

SECTION I.—*Trial of Members.*

1.	Christian discipline protected by civil authority	89
2.	Privileged communications	91
3.	Rights of members	92
4.	Mr. Wesley's mode of removing disorderly members	93

SECTION II.—*President of the Trial.*

1.	Preacher in charge	93
2.	President appointed by presiding elder	95

CONTENTS.

Page

3. Junior preacher incompetent........................... 96
4. Delivering a charge to the committee.................. 96

SECTION III.—*Complaint.*

1. Committee of investigation........................... 96
2. Bill of charges....................................... 97
3. Insufficient evidence................................. 97
4. Period within which responsible...................... 98
5. What is indictable................................... 98
6. Accessories to crime................................. 98
7. Mode of drawing bill of charges...................... 99
8. Object of formal charges............................. 99
9. What the charge must involve........................ 100
10. Correspondence between charges and specifications... 100
11. How expressed....................................... 100
12. Different crimes to be separately given 101
13. To what extent specific............................. 101
14. What errors no bar to the proceedings............... 101
15. By whom charges are to be signed 102
16. When to be signed by the pastor..................... 102
17. When several persons are involved................... 103
18. Notification of the accused......................... 103
19. Where the notice is to be left...................... 104

SECTION IV.—*Select Committee.*

1. Who eligible... 104
2. By whom appointed.................................... 104
3. Character of the committee........................... 105
4. Duty of the committee................................ 106
5. Verdict to be based on testimony..................... 107
6. Making up judgment................................... 107
7. Relation of the presiding officer to the committee... 109
8. Ambiguous or equivocal terms........................ 110
9. Females entitled to vote 110

SECTION V.—*The Trial.*

1. Duty of the presiding officer....................... 110
2. Mode of conducting a trial.......................... 111
3. Confession of guilt................................. 112
4. Refusing to answer.................................. 112

CONTENTS.   13

	Page
5. Second indictment	112
6. Plea of non-reception	113
7. Plea in abatement	113
8. New issues	113
9. Ruling out specifications	114
10. Adjournment by presiding officer	114
11. Immaterial facts	115
12. Evading a trial	115
13. Limited to the charge	115
14. Refusing to entertain bill of charges	116
15. Dismissing the case	116
16. Counsel to be restricted to the members of the Church	116
17. Where the trial should be held	117
18. Testimony not to be erased without consent	117
19. Delivering a charge on trials of preachers	117

Section VI.—*General Laws of Evidence.*

1. Should be understood......................... 117
2. First rule, evidence correspond to the allegation........ 118
3. Second rule, sufficient if the substance be proved...... 118
4. Third rule, obligation of proving lies upon the complainant... 119
5. Fourth rule, the best evidence must be produced....... 120
6. Hearsay evidence................................. 120
7. When it is to be admitted......................... 121

Section VII.—*Witnesses.*

1. Number of witnesses 121
2. Party in the suit................................ 122
3. Husband and wife................................ 122
4. Incompetent witnesses........................... 123
5. Atheists 123
6. "Witnesses from without"........................ 124
7. Admissibility a question of law 124
8. The pastor as a witness.......................... 124

Section VIII.—*Examination of Witnesses.*

1. By whom first examined.......................... 125
2. Examined out of each other's hearing 125
3. Mode of giving testimony........................ 125
4. Leading questions............................... 125

	Page
5. Writing their testimony	126
6. Impression and belief	126
7. Correction of testimony	127
8. When exceptions should be taken	127
9. Refusing to answer	127
10. Questions by presiding officers	127
11. Putting under oath	127
12. Evidence of good character	128
13. Impeachment of witnesses	128

Section IX.—*Depositions.*

1. When to be taken	129
2. Notification	129
3. Form of notice	130
4. Form of deposition	130
5. Should be sealed up	131
6. *Ex parte* deposition	131
7. Commission at conference	132
8. Part of a deposition	132

Section X.—*Appeal.*

1. Privilege of appeal	132
2. Whether it can be entertained	133
3. Bar to appeal	133
4. No appeal from record of withdrawal	134
5. When to be taken	134
6. Imperfect records	135
7. Records not signed	135
8. Mode of conducting appeals	136
9. Admitting appeals	136
10. Power of appellate courts	138
11. Decisions of appellate courts	138
12. New evidence	139
13. Relation of expelled members whose cases have been remanded	139
14. Quarterly conference cannot reopen a case after an appeal is taken	140
15. Effect of reversing a decision	140
16. Restoration of official relation	140
17. When a decision is final	141
18. Relation of a person who has taken an appeal	141

CONTENTS. 15

	Page
9. Appeals to be entered on the records	142
20. Prosecuting appeals	142
21. Power of presiding officer in case of appeals	142
22. May change the venue on demand of either party	143

Section XI.—*New Trial.*

1. By what authority granted 143
2. Right of the pastor 143
3. Steps to be taken 143
4. When to be allowed 144

Section XII.—*Trial of Local Preachers.*

1. Ministerial responsibility 145
2. When a committee to be called 145
3. Number of the committee 146
4. Who may constitute the committee 147
5. Mode of conducting the investigation 147
6. By whom suspended 147
7. Acquittal no bar to subsequent trial 148
8. Mode of conducting the trial 148
9. What testimony to be admitted 148
10. Trial in the absence of the accused 149
11. Punishment awarded by quarterly conference 148
12. Limit of quarterly conference action 149
13. When the decision to be given 150
14. Charges not to be altered 150
15. Not self-accuser 150
16. Case before the civil tribunal 150
17. Counsel not disqualified as members 151
18. Rule under which the case is brought 152

Section XIII.—*Trial of Traveling Preachers.*

1. Nature of investigating committees 152
2. Of what offenses take cognizance 152
3. Reference at the annual conference 153
4. Reference to the presiding elder for examination 154
5. Acquittal by the committee no bar to subsequent trial.. 154
6. By whom suspended 155
7. Committee when conferences are divided 155
8. Powers of presiding officer in the examination of a presiding elder 155

CONTENTS.

	Page
9. Place of holding the investigation	155
10. For what offenses arrested	156
11. Form of trial	156
12. Trial in the absence of the accused	157
13. A suspended preacher cannot afterward be expelled for the same offense	157
14. Period of suspension	157
15. Location without consent	158
16. Duty of the secretary	158
17. Committee cannot sit after the final adjournment of conference	159

Section XIV.—*Church Offenses.*

1. Specific rule 159
2. The different rules 159
3. When Church labor is required 160
4. Disseminating erroneous doctrines 161
5. Mode of treating such as disseminate errors 162
6. Slander 162
7. When the truthfulness of the statement may be proved. 163
8. By whom the charge of slander must be made ... 163

Section XV.—*Penalty.*

1. Design of penalty 163
2. Different awards 164
3. Forgiveness 164
4. Censure and suspension 166
5. Period of suspension 166
6. Penalty based upon charges 166
7. Repelling from love-feasts 167
8. Penalty for maladministration 167
9. Readmission of expelled members 167
10. Restoration by the annual conference 168
11. No discretionary power given to the president after the verdict is rendered 168
12. Public confession 169
13. "Reading out" of society 169
14. Refusing to comply with the requisition of the Church.. 170

CONTENTS.

SECTION XVI.—*Arbitration.*

		Page
1.	History of the rule	170
2.	Discretionary power of the pastor	171
3.	Definition of terms	171
4.	Arbiters members of the Church	171
5.	President of the arbitration	172
6.	Mode of conducting an arbitration	172
7.	When required to arbitrate	172
8.	Dispute with a corporation	173
9.	Refusing to arbitrate	173
10.	Lawsuits	173
11.	Accounts of those " who fail in business "	173

CHAPTER VI.
CHURCH PROPERTY.

SECTION I.—*Building Churches and Parsonages.*

1. Pecuniary liabilities.................................. 175
2. Personal liability of the building committee............ 176
3. Liability when they exceed the estimated expense...... 177

SECTION II.—*Trustees.*

1. By whom Church property is held................... 177
2. Mode of creating trustees............................ 179
3. Who are eligible as trustees.......................... 179
4. Limitations of power................................ 180
5. Entitled to possession................................ 181
6. For what purposes only the church can be used........ 182
7. Trustees of an unincorporated society................ 182
8. Term of office....................................... 182
9. Powers of trustees and stewards..................... 183
10. To whom responsible............................... 184
11. Powers restricted to the objects of their creation...... 184

SECTION III.—*Pews.*

1. Legal rights of pew owners.......................... 184
2. Right of occupancy on all public occasions........... 186

CONTENTS.

	Page
3. Restriction of rights	187
4. When a right expires	187
5. Contract for a pew must be written	188
6. Pews as real or personal estate	188
7. Exempt from taxation	188
8. Selling pews at auction	189
9. Form of deed of a pew	189

Section IV.—*Subscription Papers.*

1. To whom made payable	190
2. When payment must be demanded	191
3. Conditional subscriptions	191
4. Fictitious subscriptions	192
5. Deductions by the collector	192
6. When not collectable	192

CHAPTER VII.

MINISTERIAL SUPPORT.

Section I.—*Allowance.*

1. Salaries at different periods	193
2. Support and supplies	193
3. Fifth collection	198
4. Chartered fund	199
5. Traveling expenses of preachers	199
6. Traveling expenses of editors	199
7. Estimating committee	200
8. Appropriations to those in debt to the Book Concern	201
9. Supply of the pulpit during the session of the annual conference	201
10. Absent on official business	201
11. Serving a corporation or benevolent institution	201
12. Suspension cuts off claim	202
13. Widow's claim	202
14. Adopted children	202

CONTENTS.

SECTION II.—*Stewards.*

	Page
1. Origin of stewards	203
2. Their duties	203
3. By whom appointed	207
4. To whom responsible	207
5. Recording stewards	207
6. Resignation of office	208
7. Stewards when two circuits are united	208

CHAPTER VIII.

RULES OF ORDER.

1. Parliamentary rules	209
2. Temporary organization	209
3. Permanent organization	211
4. Presiding officer	211
5. Secretary	213
6. Members	215
7. Motions	216
8. Indefinite postponement	217
9. Laying on the table	217
10. Referring to a committee	218
11. Division of a question	218
12. Filling blanks	219
13. Amendments	219
14. Privileged questions	222
15. Adjournment	222
16. Orders of the day	223
17. Incidental questions	224
18. Questions of order	224
19. Previous question	225
20. Order of proceeding	226
21. Order in debate	228
22. Taking the question	230
23. Reconsideration	231
24. Committees	232
25. Reports of committees	233
26. Minority report	233
27. Committee of the whole	234
28. Rules of the General Conference of 1884	236

CHAPTER IX.

FORMULAS.

SECTION I.—*Formulas for Preachers in Charge.*

	Page
1. Note of recommendation to a member	248
2. Exhorter's license	249
3. Recommendation to a local preacher	249
4. Class-book	250
5. Church register for a successor	250
6. Register of the children	250
7. Collections for benevolent objects	251
8. Steward's certificate	251
9. Benevolent institutions	251
10. Wills	252

SECTION II.—*Formulas for Presiding Elders.*

1. License of a local preacher...... 254
2. Recommendation to the traveling connection...... 254
3. Recommendation for deacon or elder's orders...... 255
4. Recommendation for recognition of orders...... 256
5. Recommendation for restoration of credentials...... 256
6. Superannuated preacher's certificate...... 257

A GUIDE-BOOK

IN THE

ADMINISTRATION OF THE DISCIPLINE.

CHAPTER I.
CHURCH MEMBERSHIP.

SECTION I.—*Members.*

1. THE regularly-constituted pastor is the proper authority to admit suitable persons to the communion of the Church. The preacher in charge, acting at first under the authority of Mr. Wesley, received members into the society, and severed their relations from the Church, according to his own convictions of duty. In 1784 the assistant was restricted from giving tickets to any, until they had been recommended by a leader with whom they had met, at least two months, on trial. In 1789 the term of probation was extended to six months. In 1836 the phrase, "give tickets to none," was changed to "let none be received into the Church."

Hence, since the organization of our Church, none could be received into full communion who had not previously been recommended by a leader; and, since 1840, it has been required that the applicant pass a satisfactory examination before the Church, respecting the correctness of his doctrine and his willingness to observe the rules of the Church.

2. Membership in a Christian Church should never depend upon the result of a vote; and yet, if any member of the Church is not satisfied, with the evidence presented, of the moral and Christian character of the candidate, he should have an opportunity to make objections to his reception. In no case, however, should the reception of a person be a matter of public debate before the Church. When it is known that objections exist, the reception of the person should be postponed, and private measures adopted which will secure the purity and peace of the Church.

3. It is unfavorable to good government in the Church for a preacher, under any circumstances, to receive into membership, in his charge, a person living in the bounds of another pastoral charge; yet established usage justifies

it under some circumstances, especially in cities, where there are separate charges, and where it is difficult to define them geographically. But, in these circumstances, comity and Christian courtesy should be strictly maintained. It is possible that there may be cases of mere prejudice, without any tangible cause, that might render one society unwilling to admit a person to membership which would not be a sufficient reason for preventing him from joining another society; but when responsible members of the society where the person lives present specific objections to the reception of the person in another society, especially if the objection grows out of former Church relations, or the disciplinary action of the Church, the person should not be received until satisfaction is made to the aggrieved society. (Bishop Janes.)

4. "If a member has been expelled according to due disciplinary forms, and, without changing his residence, should go to another Methodist society and join on trial, it would be maladministration for the preacher, at the expiration of six months, to receive such a person into the Church, provided that no satisfaction had been given to the society which arraigned him; for the Discipline expressly declares: 'After such

forms of trial and expulsion, such persons shall have no privileges of society, or of sacraments, in our Church, without confession, contrition, and satisfactory reformation.' "—*Bps. Waugh and Janes.*

5. A member who has withdrawn, or been expelled from our Church, and who never afterward connected himself with another evangelical Church, cannot again be received unless he joins on trial, as in the first instance.

6. " If a member in good standing in any other orthodox evangelical Church shall desire to unite with us, such applicant may, by giving satisfactory answers to the usual inquiries, be received at once into full membership." The society must decide what is evidence of " good standing in other orthodox Churches." Letters of dismission and recommendation are not necessarily required, as some denominations never grant such, unless they are to be presented to sister Churches of their own denomination. Such persons, however, should certify the Churches of which they have been members of their intention to join another Church, and of their consequent withdrawal.

7. By "*orthodox*" or *evangelical Churches* are

meant those whose doctrinal creed embraces, especially, the divinity and atonement of our Lord Jesus Christ, the depravity of the human heart, justification by faith alone, regeneration by the Holy Ghost, the witness of the Spirit, and future rewards and punishments, and whose communicants generally are reputed to be devout and Christian men.

8. The following law decision was rendered by the General Conference of 1860:

"1. If a preacher in charge of any work receive a person into the Church contrary to the Discipline can the Annual Conference correct the administration, and declare that the person, having been received contrary to Discipline, is therefore not a member?

"*Answer.* No. This question was decided by the General Conference of 1852 by the adoption of the following resolution:

"*Resolved,* That when an Annual Conference decides that a preacher having charge has received or expelled a member contrary to the Discipline, the decision does not exclude the member so received, but restores the member so expelled. (General Conference Journal, page 73.)"—*Gen. Conf. Jour.,* p. 297.

See also Appendix to Dis. of 1884, ¶ 537, §§ 1, 2.

Section II.—*Probationers.*

1. If the visible Church of Christ is a congregation of faithful men, in which the pure word of God is preached and the sacraments duly administered, as our Articles of Religion teach, it is a matter of vital importance to test, with deep scrutiny, the moral and Christian character of those who propose to enter her holy communion. No proselyte was admitted to Jewish fellowship without being well proved and instructed. The same care was observed by the early Christian Church. "None in those days," says Lord King, "were hastily advanced to the higher forms of Christianity, but, according to their knowledge and merit, gradually arrived thereto." Bishop Stillingfleet remarks that one principal cause "of the great flourishing of religion in the primitive times was the strictness used by them in their admission of members" into Church fellowship. Origen, in his treatise against Celsus, remarks that "they did inquire into the lives and carriages to discern their seriousness in the profession of Christianity during their being catechumens;" and if they evinced true repentance and reformation of life, they were then admitted to a participation of the mysteries.

2. It is the prerogative of the preacher in charge alone to receive persons on trial. No one whose name is taken by a class-leader can be considered as a member on trial until the preacher recognizes him as such.

3. The only condition required of those joining on trial is, "a desire to flee from the wrath to come, and to be saved from their sins." (¶ 31.) This desire, however, must be evinced "by doing no harm, by avoiding evil of every kind," "by doing good," "by instructing, reproving, or exhorting all they have any intercourse with," "by running with patience the race which is set before them, denying themselves, and taking up their cross daily, submitting to bear the reproach of Christ, to be as the filth and offscouring of the world, and looking that men should say all manner of evil of them falsely, for the Lord's sake," and "by attending upon all the ordinances of God." As the minister may not know whether the candidate makes a truthful declaration of his moral state, he is directed to exercise "great care" in "receiving persons on trial," and to enroll no one unless he gives evidence of "earnest desire to be saved from his sins." As the candidate is not supposed, at the time of joining on trial, to be acquainted with our doctrines, usages, and

discipline, he is not required, at that time, to subscribe to our articles of religion and general economy; but if he proposes to join in full connection, " he must give satisfactory assurances both of the correctness of his faith and his willingness to observe and keep the rules of the Church." (¶ 48, § 3.) A probationer enters into no covenant with the Church. Every step he takes is preliminary to this, and either party may, at any time, quietly dissolve the relation between them without rupture or specific Church labor.

4. The Discipline does not specify the time when the probation shall close, but it has fixed its least period. "Let no one be received into full membership until such person has been *at least six months on trial.*" (¶ 48, § 3.) If either party desires a longer probation, a judicious administrator will readily allow it. A Church relation is so sacred and intimate that it should not be formed if there are secret misgivings on either party. The hand of fellowship, when given, should be hearty, sincere, and deeply affectionate. But, when both parties are satisfied, and the usual period of probation has expired, the candidate should be advised to consummate his full connection with the Church.

as a duty which he owes to the great Head of the Church and to the world.

5. A member on trial is entitled to the special watch-care of the Church; he has a right to attend its general religious meetings, its class-meetings, and love-feasts.

A probationer is not entitled to hold any official relation, as steward, class-leader, exhorter, or local preacher. Where a new society has just been organized, necessity may compel the preacher to appoint some probationer to take charge of the class, but such an appointment does not give the person a connection with the quarterly conference. None can form a part of this important judicatory of our Church who has never entered into covenant with us, or signified his " willingness to observe and keep the rules of the Church."

Nor is it the order of the Church for probationers, who have never been baptized, to partake of the holy sacrament. The initiatory rite should first be administered before the person is admitted to all the distinguishing rites of the new covenant.

6. A person on trial cannot be arraigned before the society, or a select number of them, on

definite charges and specifications. "If he walk disorderly, he is passed out by the door at which he came in. The pastor, upon the evidence and recommendation required in the Discipline, entered his name as a candidate, or probationer, for membership, and placed him in a class for religious training and improvement; now, if his conduct be contrary to the Gospel, or, in the language of our rule, if he 'walk disorderly and will not be reproved,' it is the duty of the pastor to discontinue him, to erase his name from the class-book and probationers' list. This is not to be done rashly, or on suspicion, or slight evidence of misconduct. It is made the duty of his leader to report weekly to his pastor 'any that walk disorderly and will not be reproved.' This implies that the leader, on discovering an impropriety in his conduct, first conversed privately with him, and, on finding that he had done wrong, attempted to administer suitable reproof that he might be recovered. Had he received reproof, this had been the end of the matter; but he 'would not be reproved'— would not submit to reproof—and the leader therefore reports the case to the pastor. But it is evidently the design that after this first failure on the part of the leader, further efforts should be made by the pastor; for the rule, after pro-riding that such conduct shall be made known to the pastor, adds: 'We will admonish him of the error of his ways. We will bear with him for a season. But, then, if he repent not, he hath no more place among us.' The pastor, on consultation with the leader and others when convenient in country societies, and with the leaders' meeting, where there is one, determines on the proper course, and carries the determination into effect. Here is a just correspondence between rights and duties."—*Plat. Meth.*, p. 87.

SECTION III.— *Withdrawal.*

1. Church relation, from the nature of the case, must depend upon the mutual pleasure of the parties. No Church covenant ought to be construed into a solemn pledge and obligation to remain during life with that particular branch of the Church of Christ with which the person first unites. It may, indeed, be deemed a solemn pledge to remain in fellowship with some branch of the visible Church. Dissatisfaction with the doctrines or polity of a Church, after long and prayerful examination, may be a sufficient reason why a new Church relationship should be formed.

2. As Church relationship is formed to promote the mutual holiness of its members, and more successfully to extend Christianity through the world, the Church can never be a party to the removal of a member so long as he discharges faithfully his covenant vows. As it was voluntary for the person to enter this relation, so it is optional with him to withdraw from this connection whenever he is disposed, provided he has faithfully discharged his obligations. But if he determines to withdraw, " he shall communicate his purpose to the preacher in charge." The Church may labor to show him the folly and indiscretion of the act, but, if he persists in his determination, the Church must give her consent; but the acquiescence of the Church is not to be deemed as an assumption of a part of the responsibility of the act.

3. When a Church relation is formed, the member, virtually, promises to observe the rules and usages of the society, and if he violates them, to submit to the discipline of the Church. And hence none can claim a withdrawal from the Church against whom charges have been preferred, or until the Church has had an opportunity to recognize the withdrawal. A solemn covenant cannot be dissolved until the parties

are duly notified. The bishops have unanimously declared that "the admission of the right to withdraw at option, without the consent of the Church, especially when under imputation of gross and scandalous offences, would operate most injuriously to the maintenance of wholesome discipline and sound morals. In accordance with this view, we deem it to be our duty to say that it is contrary to the economy and usage of the Methodist Episcopal Church to allow ministers or members, when guilty of gross violations of the Discipline, to evade its salutary authority and force by declaring themselves withdrawn from the jurisdiction of the Church." (1848.)

4. But, though no accused member can claim *the right to withdraw*, yet the body to which he is responsible may " suffer " an accused member " to withdraw from the Church, should he request it, before the trial takes place." " For scandalous crimes," says Bishop Hedding, "expulsion should undoubtedly take place," and if the authorities of the Church should proceed and expel a member who had violated his Church covenant, and declared himself beyond the pale of the Church, they would be protected by the civil law, provided their action was in

accordance with the rules of the Church. The Church must decide when her purity and influence demand the expulsion of disorderly members from her communion. (Gen. Conf. Jour., 1848, p. 129.)

5. When several members of our Church withdraw in a body from our public and social meetings, and the oversight of the pastor, and appoint separate meetings for themselves, they are not to be considered as withdrawn from the Church, but they may be summoned, each separately, to answer for neglect of duty and disobedience to the order of the Church. "No member of our Church can be pronounced withdrawn from the Church without at least his verbal consent, so as to preclude the member from Church privileges, or the right of trial if he desires it."—*Gen. Conf. Jour.*, 1860, p. 428.

6. If a member makes an application to withdraw, and after a few days expresses a desire to remain in the Church, if the withdrawal has not been announced, and no entry has been made on the Church books, it is optional with the Church either to declare him withdrawn, or to allow him to recall his request. But if the withdrawal has been consummated by the as-

sent of the Church, and the registry of the fact, it cannot be annulled by Church action. (Bp. Janes.)

7. A member who refuses to attend to his duties, to meet in class, etc., does not by that act withdraw from the Methodist Episcopal Church. But such member is responsible to the Church for such violation of his Church covenant.

8. When a minister desires to withdraw from the Methodist Episcopal Church, his request must be presented to the body to which he is responsible. When a superannuated preacher resides beyond the bounds of his Annual Conference, a presiding elder cannot give him a certificate of withdrawal. (Gen. Conf. Jour., 1864, p. 141.)

CHAPTER II.
THE CONFERENCES.

SECTION I.—*Annual Conferences.*

1. The first Annual Conference in England was held at the Foundry in London, June, 1744, at which the following persons were present:— John Wesley, Charles Wesley, John Hodges, Rector of Wenvo, Henry Piers, Vicar of Bexley, Samuel Taylor, Vicar of Quinton, and John Meriton. The first Annual Conference in America was held in Philadelphia, June, 1773, at which the Rev. Thomas Rankin presided.

2. Districts have existed not in name but in fact, since the organization of our Church. Mr. Wesley desired that "no more elders should be ordained, in the first instance, than were absolutely necessary, and that the work on the continent should be divided between them in respect to the duties of their office." The General Conference, at first, elected only twelve elders to administer the ordinances of the Church; but Bishop Asbury and the District

Conferences afterward enlarged the number, and gave them the name by which they were afterward designated. This proceeding subsequently received the approbation of Mr. Wesley and of the General Conference of 1792.

3. The term *Circuit* was first introduced into the Minutes of the conference in the year 1746. At that time a circuit embraced some fifteen or twenty societies which lay around some principal society. At each conference two, three, or four preachers were appointed to each circuit, and the one having the charge was denominated an *Assistant*, because he assisted Mr. Wesley in superintending the societies, and the other preachers were called *Helpers*. In England the name *Circuit* is now generally retained, and applied to the stations of the preachers whose spheres of ministerial labor do not extend far beyond the limits of the town in which they reside, as well as to those which spread over a much larger space. In this country, in colloquial language, the term station is applied to a charge embracing only a single worshipping congregation, and circuit to a more extended field; but, in the Discipline, these terms are frequently used interchangeably. When a society becomes, in common parlance, a *Station*, it loses no title

to funded property which it held while it was called a *Circuit*, nor do *Circuit Preachers* form a different class of beneficiaries from those who are termed *Stationed Preachers*.

4. A Bishop sustains the relation of *Moderator* to the General Conference. He represents no section or interest of the Church; he can claim no right to introduce motions, to make speeches, or to cast votes on any question. As president, he can neither form rules nor decide law questions in the General Conference; and, on mere questions of order, there is an appeal from his decision to the deliberative body. (Bishops' Address to Gen. Conf., 1840; Bishop Hedding on Discipline, p. 10.)

No one of the bishops is specially designated as the president of the General Conference. The order of presiding is a matter of mutual agreement among the bishops. He who occupies the chair for the time being is the legal president of the conference.

By a conventional arrangement among the bishops, there is properly but one official president of an annual conference, though other bishops may preside and assist in all the duties of the chair. No bishop has a right to make a motion, to vote, or to make speeches on controverted questions in an annual conference.

5. The peculiar prerogatives of the president of an annual conference are the following:

a. He may adjourn the conference over which he presides when, in his judgment, all the business prescribed by the Discipline shall have been transacted, provided that the conference shall be allowed to sit, at least, a week, and also provided, that if an exception shall be taken, by the conference, to his so adjourning it, the exception shall be entered upon the journals of the conference. (Gen. Conf. Jour., 1840, p. 121.)

b. The bishop must decide all questions of law involved in proceedings pending in an annual conference, and all questions of order raised in the ordinary business of the conference. On a question of law, an appeal may be taken, either by the conference as a body, or by any member of it, to the next ensuing General Conference. The decision of the president, however, must be made the basis of action, for the time being, by the conference. On a question of order, an appeal may be taken at the time to the annual conference.

c. The president of an annual, a district, or

a quarterly conference has the right to decline putting the question on a motion, resolution, or report, when, in his judgment, such motion, resolution, or report does not relate to the proper business of the conference. Provided, that in all such cases, the president, on being required to do so, shall have inserted in the journals of the conference his refusal to put the question on such motion, resolution, or report, with his reasons for so refusing; and also provided, that when an annual conference shall differ from the president on a question of law, it shall have a right to record its dissent on the journals, provided there shall be no discussion on the subject. (Gen. Conf. Jour., 1840, p. 121.)

d. The following decisions were made by the General Conference of 1860:

"1. If a motion is made in an annual or quarterly conference, which, if passed, would be a positive violation of Discipline, should the president put the motion and allow the Discipline to be set aside, or what should he do?

"*Ans.* He should refuse to put the motion.

"The president of an annual or a quarterly meeting Conference has the right to decline putting the question on a motion, resolution, or report, when, in his judgment, such motion, resolution, or report does not relate to the proper business of the conference." (*Gen. Conf. Jour.*, 1840, p. 121.)

This decision was made before the law for *district* conferences was enacted, but by parity of reason the rule also applies to the president of a district conference.

"2. When a bishop presiding in an annual conference decides a question of law by request of the conference, if a motion is made which would reverse the decision of the bishop, under the plea that the conference has the right to apply the law in the case, should the motion be put, and the conference be allowed to set aside the law under the pretense of applying it?

"*Ans.* No. When a question of law has been decided by a bishop in an annual conference that decision cannot be reversed or set aside except by the action of the ensuing General Conference, to which body an appeal may be taken by the annual conference or by any member thereof."—*Gen. Conf. Jour.*, 1860, p. 297.

6. No preacher having the charge of a circuit is authorized to divide, or in any way to lessen, the circuit. (Gen. Conf., 1816.)

7. In regard to episcopal decisions, the General Conference has adopted the following sentiments:

"*Whereas*, under the rule which says, 'A bishop shall decide all questions of law in an annual conference, subject to an appeal to the General Conference,' a custom has grown up of evoking episcopal decisions touching the administration of the Discipline outside of the annual conferences; and,

"*Whereas*, the opinions of the bishops, given in writing in the intervals of the annual conferences, are sometimes regarded as decisions of law, binding in the administration of Discipline; and,

"*Whereas*, these decisions and opinions are sometimes in conflict with each other, springing up from questions growing out of peculiar and ever-varying circumstances; and,

"*Whereas*, it is the judgment of this Conference that the use made of the rule aforesaid was not intended by the General Conference which established it, that General Conference intending it for the administration of the conferences, and not of the individual pastors; therefore,

"1. *Resolved*, That every administrator of the Discipline is responsible to the proper authorities for his administration of the rules of the Church, and may not plead episcopal decisions as law.

"2. *Resolved,* That while the counsels of our superintendents are to be highly respected, and to be considered of great value in the administration of Discipline, their decisions are not to be regarded as having the force of *law* outside of the annual conferences."—*Gen. Conf. Jour.*, 1860, p. 428.

" That we deem it inexpedient for a Bishop presiding at an annual conference to render formal decisions of questions of law presented on fictitious cases, and where the subject is not involved in the proceedings pending, nor should any such decisions be entered upon the conference journals."—*Gen. Conf. Jour.*, 1868.

8. The conference year commences when the appointments are announced in the annual conference, and continues until the announcing of the appointments at the next ensuing conference. (Bishop Waugh.)

9. The General Conference of 1860 has given the following instructions in regard to special transfers :

"1. *Resolved,* That while we cheerfully accord to our excellent superintendents their constitutional right to supply the general work by transfers when necessary, we respectfully request that transfers may never be made solely at the personal solicitation of the preacher desiring to be transferred, nor yet to gratify the wishes of any one charge between whom and the proposed appointee negotiations may have been previously made.

"2. *Resolved*, That negotiations for special appointments in the pastoral work between individual ministers and societies, prior to the exercise of the regular appointing power in our Church, is contrary to our economy and injurious to our itinerant system."—*Gen. Conf. Jour.*, 1860, p. 398.

10. All the preachers, whether in full connection or on probation, are required to be present at the annual conference and undergo the required examinations. If a local deacon or elder, or if a minister from another evangelical denomination, join the traveling connection, he is required to pass the four years' course of study.

11. "Can a traveling preacher, during the interval of the annual conference of which he

is a member, be suspended for refusing to attend to the work assigned him?

"*Ans.* It is the duty of a presiding elder 'to take charge of all the elders and deacons in his district,' and to 'take care that every part of our Discipline be enforced.' Now our Discipline provides (¶¶ 176, 182) that no elder or deacon who ceases to travel without the consent of the annual conference, certified under the hand of the president of the conference, except in case of sickness, debility, or other unavoidable circumstances, shall on any account exercise the peculiar functions of his office, or even be allowed to preach among us.' Hence, any elder or deacon who refuses to go to the work assigned him ('except in cases of sickness,' etc.) may be suspended 'in the interval of the annual conference;' but the '*final* determination in all such cases is with' the conference."—*Gen. Conf. Jour.*, 1860, p. 297.

12. The General Conference ordered that in receiving preachers into full connection the examination of the candidates before the conference shall precede the action of conference in admitting them to full connection and electing them to orders. (Gen. Conf. Jour., p. 224.)

13. When a member of an annual conference in good standing, demands a location, the conference is obliged to grant it to him. But if the member is indebted to the Book Concern, the conference may require him to secure the debt before they grant his request. (Rec. Gen. Conf., 1840, p. 107. Also ¶ 365, Dis., 1884.)

14. The location of a traveling preacher is to be reckoned from the final adjournment of the conference session, and not from the particular time that the vote of location is taken.

15. A located preacher is entitled to a certificate of location under the hand of the president of the conference. (Gen. Conf. Jour., 1848, p. 98.)

16. A preacher who has been located, either with or without his consent, may, at any session, be readmitted to his former standing, at the option of a majority of the conference.

17. But if a preacher has withdrawn from an annual conference, he cannot again be readmitted without the usual probation, though he has returned to the Church, and his credential have been restored to him.

18. Properly accredited ministers from any branch of the Methodist Church, or from any Church agreeing with us in doctrine, may on their credentials be at once received into full connection in the traveling ministry, provided they give satisfaction to an annual conference of their literary qualifications and of their willingness to conform to our Church government and usages. (Gen. Conf. Jour., 1864, pp. 240, 241, 417.)

19. Ministers from other evangelical Churches must be recommended by some quarterly conference, according to our usages, before they can be received on trial in the traveling connection.

20. A superannuated preacher possesses all the rights, powers, and prerogatives of an effective preacher in an annual conference. He may serve on any committee, vote on any question, and represent an annual conference as a delegate in the General Conference. And whether he resides within or without the bounds of the conference of which he is a member, he is entitled to a seat in the quarterly conference, and to all the privileges of membership in the Church where he resides.

21. A preacher on trial cannot sustain a superannuated relation.

22. A bishop is not authorized to continue a preacher in a circuit or station where he has held a pastoral relation over a majority of the charge for three consecutive years, even though the station may be divided into two or more circuits or stations. (Gen. Conf. Jour., 1836, p. 473.) "Nevertheless, if in any case the term of three years shall expire in the interim of an annual conference, he may continue him until the next session, provided the time shall not be more than six months."(Discip. 1884, ¶ 164, § 3.)

23. Every preacher belonging to the traveling connection, unless he sustains a superannuated or supernumerary relation, or at the request of his Conference has been permitted to attend school, or is under arrest of character, must receive an appointment to some station recognized by our economy. Previously to 1836 preachers were frequently returned on the Minutes as being left without an appointment at their own request ; but the General Conference has forbidden the practice, except in the case of supernumerary preachers.

24. Preachers on trial who have been employed "two successive years in the regular itinerant work on circuits, in stations, or in our institutions of learning," and have satisfactorily passed the prescribed examinations, are eligible

to admission into full connection. (Dis. 1884, ¶ 158.)

25. While a preacher is on trial the annual conference alone has jurisdiction over the question of his authority to preach, and his continuance on trial is equivalent to a renewal of his license to preach, (Discipline, ¶ 154;) but if accused of crime, he is accountable to the quarterly conference of the circuit, or to the district conference within whose bounds his charge is embraced. (Dis. 1884, ¶ 223.)

26. When an annual conference requests a superintendent to appoint a preacher to a literary institution, it does not render it obligatory upon the bishop to comply with the request. (Gen. Conf. Jour., 1840, p. 165.)

"27. When a preacher is transferred from one conference to another his rights, privileges, and responsibilities in the conference to which he is transferred shall date from the date of his transfer, unless it be especially provided otherwise by the bishop by whom the transfer is made.

"But it will not be lawful for him to vote twice on the same constitutional question, or be counted twice in the same year as the basis of the election of delegates to the General Conference, nor vote for delegates to the General

Conference in any conference where he is not counted as a part of the basis of representation."—*Gen. Conf. Jour.*, 1860, p. 364; see also ¶ 541, Discipline of 1884.

SECTION II.—*District Conferences.*

1. District conferences are to be held in those districts, and in those only, in which the quarterly conferences of a majority of the circuits and stations shall have approved the law creating district conferences; which approval must be expressed by asking the presiding elder to convene a district conference according to the provisions of the law. After such approval it becomes the duty of the presiding elder to convene a district conference, and thereafter it will not be lawful for any quarterly conference in which a district conference shall be held to exercise any of the powers belonging to the district conference. (¶ 97 of Dis., 1884.)

2. District conferences are composed of all the traveling and local preachers, the exhorters, the district stewards, one Sunday-school superintendent, and one class-leader from each pastoral charge in the district. If there shall be two or more superintendents in any circuit or station, then the quarterly conference of that circuit or station shall determine which super-

intendent and which class-leader shall be a member of the district conference.

3. The district conference meets once or twice in each conference year, as each district conference shall determine. The presiding elder appoints both the time and place for the meeting held first after the approval of the law in any given district; and thereafter he appoints the time, and the district conference the place, of its subsequent meetings.

4. The presiding elder is the president of the district conference, unless a bishop be present; but in the absence of both bishop and presiding elder, the conference elects its own president by ballot from among the traveling elders.

5. The bishop or presiding elder must decide all questions of law. An appeal, however, may be taken from such decision — if given by a bishop, to the General Conference; if by an elder, to the presiding bishop of the ensuing annual conference.

6. The district conference takes cognizance of all the local preachers and exhorters in the district, and inquires respecting the gifts, labors, and usefulness of each by name, and arranges at each meeting a plan of appointments for them until the next meeting of the conference. The district conference also hears complaints against

local preachers, and tries, suspends, deprives of ministerial office and credentials, expels or acquits, any local preacher against whom charges may be preferred.

7. The district conference has authority to license local preachers and exhorters, to annually renew their licenses, and to recommend to the annual conference local preachers as suitable candidates for deacons and elders' orders, and for admission on trial in the traveling connexion; but the district conference may not so license or recommend any person without the recommendation of the quarterly conference, or of the leaders and stewards' meeting of the circuit or station of which he is a member. And in all cases the candidate must pass a satisfactory examination in doctrine and discipline. The district conference is also invested with the powers given to the quarterly conference in ¶¶ 160, 161 of the Discipline, relating to recognition of orders.

8. It is the duty of the district conference to inquire if the collections for the benevolent institutions of the Church are properly attended to in all the circuits and stations, and to adopt suitable measures for promoting their success; to inquire into the condition of the Sunday-schools in the district, and adopt suitable meas-

ures for insuring their success; to inquire respecting opportunities for missionary and Church extension enterprises within the district, and to take measures for the occupation of any neglected portions of its territories by mission Sunday-schools and appointments for public worship; to provide for appropriate religious and literary exercises during its sessions; and to take the general oversight of all the temporal and spiritual affairs of the district, subject to the provisions of the Discipline.

9. The minutes of a district conference must be read and approved at the close of the session.

10. A district conference may be discontinued by a vote of two thirds of the members present at any regular session, (notice thereof having been given at a previous session,) and with the concurrence of three fourths of the quarterly conferences in the district.

SECTION III.—*Quarterly Conferences.*

1. It is uncertain at what time quarterly conferences were introduced into our economy, but it is known that they were held at a very early period. The Large Minutes were first published in 1763, in which it is declared to be one of the numerous duties of the assistant to hold quarterly meetings, and diligently inquire

therein into the spiritual and temporal state of each society. At a very early date Mr. Wesley adopted the plan of quarterly visitations of the classes, at which he inquired into the religious state of each individual, and gave suitable pastoral advice, and renewed the certificate of membership by giving each a society ticket. The visitations were so arranged as to terminate with the four quarter-days in the national calendar; and the quarterly meetings of the circuits were appointed to be held on those days, or as near as practicable.

2. The powers of the quarterly conference are various, and, as detailed in this section, and as set forth in ¶¶ 98–104 of the Discipline, they are powers all of which may be exercised by any quarterly conference which does not belong to a district within which a district conference is held in pursuance of the provision of the Discipline in the premises. Some of the powers hitherto belonging to quarterly conferences have been transferred from the quarterly conferences to the district conferences in cases where such district conferences are held; and the powers thus transferred may not thenceforth be exercised by the quarterly conferences. In all other cases the powers of the quarterly conferences remain as heretofore provided.

3. The quarterly conference, where no district conference is held, is a court holding original jurisdiction over accused local elders, deacons, and preachers, and of preachers on trial in the traveling connexion, and a court of appeals to the laity. It is a council to constitute and appoint local preachers, to examine their moral and Christian characters, to renew their license annually, and to recommend suitable persons for ministerial orders, according to the provisions of the Discipline. It is also intrusted with the election of the stewards, and the confirmation of the Sunday-school superintendent, and the choice of the superintendent and class-leader to represent the conference in the district conference. It holds, also, a supervisory relation to the various financial and benevolent enterprises of the Church. It is authorized " to hear complaints " against the official acts and delinquencies of local preachers, stewards, and exhorters, and on application of the preacher in charge it has authority to order a new trial of an accused member. It may also elect trustees where the laws of the State permit. To it, also, trustees are to make an annual report. (See Discipline, ¶ 392.)

4. The quarterly conference is composed of all the traveling and local preachers, exhorters,

stewards, class-leaders, and trustees of the Churches in the circuits or stations, and of such members of the annual conference as the bishop may designate, who, as agents, editors, etc., sustain no pastoral relation to any society, and of such superannuated preachers as reside on the circuit; the first male superintendents of our Sunday-schools, said superintendents and trustees being members of our Church, and approved by the quarterly conference. All members of a quarterly conference, not under charges, (unless they have been members of a committee of trial from whose decision an appeal is taken,) have equal rights to speak and vote in such conference, except on questions affecting their own standing.

5. The presiding elder, or in his absence a traveling elder appointed by him, or in his absence the preacher in charge, shall preside in the quarterly conference.

6. When two circuits are united for quarterly meetings, the secretary of the quarterly conference should record the entire doings of the conference, and the recording steward of each circuit take a copy of such records only as relate to his respective circuit.

7. The quarterly conference is authorized to inquire into the condition of each school

or society within the bounds of the circuit or station, and to remove any superintendent who may prove to be unworthy or inefficient.

8. A quarterly conference has no authority to amend or reject a Sabbath-school report presented by the preacher in charge, according to the provisions of the Discipline; but the report should be entered upon the journals of the conference without the question being put on its adoption.

9. The presiding elder must appoint the time of holding a quarterly conference. If another person appoints it without his knowledge, it is not a legal session, even if a preacher in charge presides in it.

10. A quarterly conference may adjourn from time to time to finish any pending business; but it cannot adjourn to a distant day to take up new business which would properly belong to a future quarterly conference. (Hedding on Disc., p. 36.)

11. The president of a quarterly conference has the right to adjourn the conference over which he presides when in his judgment all the business prescribed by the Discipline to such conference shall have been transacted. But if an exception be taken by the conference to his so adjourning it, the exception must be entered

upon the journals of the conference. (Gen. Conf. Jour., 1840, p. 121.)

12. "All ministers having charge of circuits or stations should faithfully enforce the provisions of the Discipline on the subject of temperance, and every presiding elder should make it a subject of inquiry in every quarterly conference."—*General Conference Jour.*, 1860, p. 395.

13. The members present at any regularly called quarterly conference constitute a legal quorum for the transaction of business. A tie vote, in a quarterly conference, decides the question in the negative, as the presiding elder is not entitled to vote.

14. The minutes of a quarterly conference must be read and approved at the close of the session when they are taken: they cannot be approved at any subsequent session. The unrecorded action of the conference is of no legal authority.

SECTION IV.—*Leaders and Stewards' Meetings.*

1. Mr. Wesley gives the following account of the origin of class-leaders and leaders' meetings. He had long been perplexed because he had no means of learning the private character of many

of his members. "At length," says he, "while we were thinking of quite another thing, we struck upon a method for which we have had cause to bless God ever since. I was talking with several of the society in Bristol (Feb. 15, 1742) concerning the means of paying the debts there, when one stood up and said, 'Let every member of the society give a penny a week till all are paid.' Another answered, 'But many of them are poor, and cannot afford to do it.' 'Then,' said he, 'put eleven of the poorest with me, and if they can give anything, well; I will call on them weekly; and if they can give nothing, I will give for them as well as for myself. And each of you call on eleven of your neighbors weekly, receive what they give, and make up what is wanting.' It was done. In a while some of them informed me they found such and such a one did not live as he ought. It struck me immediately—'This is the thing, the very thing we have wanted so long.' I called together all the leaders of the classes, (so we used to term them and their companies,) and desired that each would make particular inquiry into the behavior of those whom he saw weekly. They did so. Many disorderly walkers were detected. Some turned from the evil of their ways; some were put away from us. Many saw it with fears, and rejoiced unto God with reverence. As soon as possible the same method was used in London and all other places." The institution of weekly leaders' meetings followed of course.

2. Leaders and stewards' meetings, from their first institution, have been composed of the traveling preachers stationed in the circuit or station, and the stewards and class-leaders of the charge. The Discipline does not recognize the office of *assistant* class-leaders. Though a member may be requested to aid a leader in the discharge of his duties, yet this relation does not entitle him to a seat in the leaders' meeting, or in the quarterly conference.

3. To define specifically the duties and prerogatives of class-leaders and of leaders' meetings, Mr. Wesley published the following rules in 1771: "That it may be more easily discerned whether the members of our societies are working out their own salvation, they are divided into little companies called classes. One person in each of these is styled the leader. It is his business, (1.) To see each person in his class once a week; to inquire how their souls prosper; to advise, reprove, comfort, or exhort them.

(2.) To receive what they are willing to give toward the expenses of the society. And, (3.) To meet the assistants and the stewards once a week. This is the whole and sole business of a leader or any number of leaders. But it is common for the assistant, in any place where several leaders are met together, to ask their advice as to any thing which concerns either the temporal or spiritual welfare of the society."

No duties are so specifically assigned to the leaders' meeting as to require their being held in all our circuits and stations; yet when they are held monthly, they are found to be eminently adapted to promote the interests of the Church.

The ordinary business of a leaders and stewards' meeting embraces the following items, (Discipline, ¶ 105.)

a. That the leaders have an opportunity "to inform the minister of any that are sick, or of any that walk disorderly and will not be reproved."

b. That the pastor may examine the several class-books, and ascertain the Christian walk and character of each member of the Church, and learn what members of the flock especially need his watch-care and counsel.

c. To inquire into the religious state of all persons on trial, and ascertain who can be recommended by the leader for admission into full connection, and who should be discontinued.

d. To direct the leaders to such a course of reading and study as shall best qualify them for their work, especially to such books as will tend to increase their knowledge of the Scriptures, and make them familiar with those passages best adapted to Christian edification.

e. To recommend suitable persons to be licensed as exhorters and local preachers.

f. That the leaders may "pay the stewards what they have received of their several classes in the week preceding." And also to hear reports from the stewards.

4. Class-leaders, as such, are responsible only to the preacher in charge, who may remove them at pleasure.

CHAPTER III.

MINISTERS.

SECTION I.—*Bishops.*

1. A BISHOP is to be constituted by the election of the General Conference, and the laying on of the hands of three bishops, or at least of one bishop and two elders.

2. The duties of a bishop are: to preside in the conferences, to form the districts and fix the appointments of the preachers, to change, receive, and suspend preachers, to ordain, and to decide questions of law in annual conferences, subject to appeal to the General Conference.

SECTION II.—*Presiding Elders.*

1. The office of presiding elder is coeval with the Methodist Episcopal Church, though this officer was not so designated until 1789, and its duties were not specifically defined until 1792.

2. The origin and nature of the office are thus given by Dr. Coke and Bishop Asbury: "When Mr. Wesley drew up a plan of government for our Church in America, he desired that no more elders should be ordained, in the first instance, than were absolutely necessary.

The General Conference accordingly elected twelve elders. Bishop Asbury and the district conferences afterward found that this order of men was so necessary that they agreed to enlarge the number, and give them the name by which they are at present called, and which is perfectly scriptural, though it is not the word used in our translation: and this proceeding afterward received the approbation of Mr. Wesley. In 1792 the General Conference, equally conscious of the necessity of having such an office among us, not only confirmed every thing that Asbury and the district conferences had done, but also drew up, or agreed to, the present section for the explanation of the nature and duties of the office."—*Coke and Asbury's Notes on the Discipline.*

3. The presiding elder is authorized to decide questions of law in a quarterly conference; but an appeal may be taken from his decision to the president of the next annual conference. If the decision of the president of the conference is not satisfactory, either party may take an appeal from this decision to the General Conference.

4. A presiding elder cannot administer discipline in any society where there is a regularly constituted pastor. If there is no preacher in charge, he may discharge all the peculiar duties of the pastorate.

5. A presiding elder has no authority to permit a traveling preacher to leave his appropriate work. If a preacher leaves his charge, the responsibility rests upon himself alone, and he must answer it at the annual conference. (Gen. Conf. Jour., 1840, p. 105.)

6. A presiding elder may remove a preacher from his charge, in the interval of conference, and assign him another station within the limits of his district; but he cannot remove him beyond the bounds of his district: his powers are wholly restricted to these limits. Nor can a presiding elder change a preacher in his district from a charge to which he has been appointed by the bishop, and appoint him to another charge to which he could not be legally appointed by the bishop. (Discipline, ¶ 171, § 3.)

7. When superannuated and local preachers are employed in the pastoral work by a presiding elder, the law of limitation of time applies to them as to effective men appointed by a bishop. (Discipline, ¶ 171, § 3.)

8. Presiding elders are required to make quarterly reports of the state of the missions within their bounds to the Corresponding Sec-

retary of the Missionary Society, and to furnish the member of the General Missionary Committee of their mission district a written statement of the condition of the missions under their care prior to the annual meeting of the committee.

9. In case of application as a missionary to preach the gospel in a foreign mission, the presiding elder of the applicant should furnish the bishop having the authority to appoint testimonials on the following particulars:—

a. Character of the applicant's piety.

b. Manner and effectiveness of his preaching.

c. His natural talents and temper, and the probability of his working happily with others.

d. His judgment, discretion, and common sense.

e. The extent and qualities of his education.

f. His habits of improving time, and of seizing opportunities of usefulness.

g. The habits of economy of himself and his family.

h. His facility of acquiring influence over others.

i. His aptness in acquiring languages.

j. His personal appearance, manners, and address.

k. His character, habits, health, and consti

tution, in view of his particular field. (Missionary Manual, p. 7.)

10. Subjects for correspondence of superintendents, especially with reference to foreign missions and missions among the Indians:—

a. The peculiar customs of the people among whom they labor.

b. Their language, habits, laws, and government.

c. Their religious views and worship.

d. The degree and character of their civilization.

e. Their views and feelings with respect to Christianity, and its progress among them, if they have made any.

f. Account of particular conversions and experiences. (Miss. Manual, p. 17.)

11. When an elder is appointed or elected president of an annual conference, he has the same prerogatives as to presiding in conference, and making out the appointments, as a bishop; but such appointment confers no prerogative, except those specified above, and these, only during the session of the conference.

Section III.—*Preacher in Charge.*

1. A preacher in charge is one who has the pastoral care of a circuit or station, by the appointment of the regularly constituted authority of the Church. He may be an elder, a deacon, an unordained preacher on trial, or a local preacher employed by the presiding elder to supply some vacancy; all appointed by competent authority possess full and equal powers as preachers in charge.

2. The duties of a preacher in charge are, to take the oversight of the junior preachers on his circuit, if there be any; to renew the love-feast tickets quarterly; to hold watch-nights and love-feasts; to permit no love-feast to last longer than one hour and a half; to appoint prayer-meetings wherever it is practicable; to appoint a fast in every society on the circuit the Friday preceding each quarterly meeting, and to make a memorandum of it on all the class-papers; to read the rules of the society, with the aid of the other preachers, once a year in every congregation, and once a quarter in every society; to enforce vigorously, but calmly, all the rules of the society; to take a regular catalogue of the societies in towns and cities as they

live in the streets; to give a note of recommendation to members removing from the circuit, and to enjoin upon those removing to obtain a recommendation; to recommend decency and cleanliness every-where; to appoint a person to receive the quarterly collections in the classes; to encourage the support of missions, by forming societies and making collections in such manner as the annual conference shall direct; to provide for the diffusion of missionary intelligence in the Church and congregation; to institute a monthly missionary prayer-meeting or lecture in each society or church and congregation, wherever practicable, and to appoint, aided by the Committee on Missions, missionary collectors; to lay before the quarterly conference, at each quarterly meeting, a written statement of the number and state of the Sunday-schools in the circuit or station, and to report the same to the annual conference; to take annual collections in each of the appointments for such objects as are directed in the Discipline; to form Sunday-schools in all our congregations where ten children can be collected for that purpose; to form Bible classes; to visit the schools as often as practicable, and to preach on the subject of Sunday-schools and religious instruction in each congregation at least once in six months; to take up a collection or raise a subscription for the purchase and distribution of tracts; to catechise the children in the Sunday-school and at special meetings appointed for that purpose; to hold quarterly meetings in the absence of the presiding elder; to give an account of his circuit every quarter to his presiding elder; to report at each quarterly meeting the names of those who have been received into the Church or excluded therefrom during the quarter; also the names of those who have been received or dismissed by certificate, and of those who have died or have withdrawn from our Church; to license proper persons to officiate as exhorters; to submit the application of all who desire a license as a local preacher to the society or leaders' meeting for a recommendation to the quarterly conference; or to the quarterly conference for recommendation to the district conference; to give a certificate of the official standing of a local preacher when applied to in case of removal; to appoint and change leaders when he sees it necessary; to nominate stewards for the confirmation of the quarterly conference; to meet the stewards and leaders frequently; to inspect the accounts of the stewards; to recommend arbitration between members when there is a dispute in reference to pecuniary affairs; to appoint a committee to inspect the accounts, contracts, and circumstances of those members who fail in business or contract debts which they are not able to pay; to call a member accused of non-payment of debt before a committee for investigation and settlement; to bring to trial and expel, according to Discipline, disorderly members; to call local preachers who have failed in business before a committee; to reprove local preachers guilty of indulging in improper tempers, words, or actions, and to call those accused of crime before an investigating committee; to report to the annual conference the number of Church members, number of deaths the past year, number of probationers, number of local preachers, number of adults baptized the past year, number of children baptized the past year, number of churches and their probable value, number of parsonages and their probable value, amount collected for superannuated preachers, amount collected for the Missionary Society, amount collected for Church Extension, amount collected for the Sunday-School Union, number of officers and teachers, number of scholars, number of volumes in library; to recommend to every class or society to raise a quarterly or annual subscription to meet the current expenses of preaching the Gospel on the circuit, and to make up the allowance of the preachers; to appoint a person to receive the quarterly collection in the classes; to take up a yearly collection, and, if expedient, a quarterly one to make up the deficiencies at the annual conference; to be collectors and receivers of subscriptions, etc., for the Chartered Fund; to supply the societies with books; to leave his successor a particular account of the circuit, including an account of the subscribers for our periodicals; to keep in a suitable book a faithful record of all the subscribers to our periodicals in his charge; enter the *date* and *amount* of payments, and leave the book for his successor, and a note of the place where it is left on the plan of the circuit; (see Gen. Conf. Jour., 1840, p. 117;) to appoint a board of trustees for holding Church property when necessary.

3. The preacher in charge who is a member of an annual conference, and a preacher on trial, are both responsible to the annual conference for their administration of discipline; and a local preacher in charge of a society is responsible to the quarterly conference.

SECTION IV.—*Local Preachers.*

1. No one can be licensed as a local preacher until the following steps have been taken :—

a. He must be recommended to the quarterly conference by the leaders and stewards' meeting, or by the society of which he is a member. It is not sufficient that he be recommended by the class of which he is a member. If the application for a license is to be made to a district conference, he must be recommended by the leaders and stewards' meeting or by the quarterly conference.

b. He must pass a satisfactory examination on the subject of doctrines and discipline.

2. The license of a local preacher is given by the quarterly or district conference, and not by the presiding elder ; and hence the license must be signed by the president of the conference, even if he is the person thus licensed.

3. A quarterly conference may refuse to renew the license of a local preacher without any impeachment of moral character, or finding any decrease of piety, talent, or usefulness. (Bishops Waugh and Janes.)

4. Every license is given for one year, and for one year only; and hence, in the interval of a conference year, a license cannot be revoked unless the quarterly or district conference, in due form, for cause assigned, deprive the local preacher of his ministerial office; and if, at the expiration of the year, no conference action is taken upon it, the license becomes null and void. The question of renewal of licenses may be laid over as unfinished business until the next succeeding quarterly conference. If the license of a local preacher has expired, the same preliminary steps must be taken to regain it as if no license had ever been given. The fact that the proper body has formerly recommended a person for local preacher's license, would impose no obligation upon it to renew the recommendation if the question were again submitted to it. If a district or quarterly conference refuses to renew the license of a local preacher, a subsequent conference cannot reconsider the question and grant a renewal.

5. The license of a local preacher "must be renewed annually" by the district or quarterly conference; but by this expression is meant that it must be renewed in every ecclesiastical rather than in every calendar year. If, by the ar-

rangement of holding quarterly conferences, the time exceeds by a few weeks the calendar year, it does not render void the license. And if a local preacher should change his residence, and it should be found that no district or quarterly conference will be held for a short time after the calendar year has expired, the license will remain in full force until the question of renewal can be submitted.

6. An ordained local preacher is not required to have his credentials renewed annually. His ordination parchments authorize him to preach until they are surrendered, or made void by Church action or a violation of ordination vows. But ordained local preachers are required to pass an examination in the quarterly or district conference respecting their gifts, labors, and usefulness. Usage requires that this examination be made annually. If a quarterly or district conference refuses to pass the character of a local elder or deacon for any alleged reason, the administrator should proceed to an investigation of the case, according to disciplinary rule.

7. No local preacher can be employed by a presiding elder to travel, except in the interval of a district or quarterly conference, without a

recommendation of such district or quarterly conference. This recommendation may be the usual recommendation to an annual conference to be received into the traveling connexion, or it may be a simple recommendation to be employed, for the time being, on a circuit or station.

8. Every local preacher is amenable to the quarterly conference where he resides, or to the district conference, for his Christian character and the faithful performance of his ministerial office; and to it he shall report his labors. If he 'has a pastoral charge, he must hold his Church relation in that charge. (Discipline, ¶ 193.) When a preacher is located, or discontinued by an annual conference, he is amenable to the district or quarterly conference of the circuit where he had his last appointment. (Discipline, ¶ 190.) A preacher on trial is "amenable for his *administration*, when he is in charge, to his presiding elder and the annual conference. The presiding elder can correct his errors and reprove him, and change his relation by putting him under another preacher; and the conference can discontinue him for that cause."—*Bp. Hedding.*

9. The following prerequisites are necessary for the ordination of a local preacher:

a. He must have held a local preacher's license for four consecutive years before his ordination.

b. He must have been examined on the subject of doctrines and discipline.

c. He must have received a "testimonial" from the quarterly or district conference, signed by the president and countersigned by the secretary. This testimonial must recommend the applicant as a suitable person to receive ministerial orders.

d. He must pass an examination of character before the annual conference, and obtain its approbation and election to orders.

The candidate for elder's orders must either certify his belief in the doctrines and discipline of our Church, with his own signature, or make this profession before the conference.

10. Wesleyan local preachers, from the British, Irish, and Canada connections, when duly received by us, are eligible to deacon's and elder's orders at the same time they would have been if they had received their first license from us; but this rule applies to none who come from other Christian Churches.

11. The recommendations of quarterly or district conferences for the ordination or admission

of local preachers into the traveling connection, on trial, are not valid after the next annual session for which they were given.

12. The presiding elders and the preachers in charge are required so to arrange the appointments, whenever it is practicable, as to give the local preachers regular and systematic employment on the Sabbath; but they cannot control the appointments of local preachers, unless they conflict with the plan of the circuit.

13. If a local preacher desires to withdraw from the Methodist Episcopal Church, his request should be presented to the quarterly or district conference to which he is amenable. The preacher in charge can take no other action in the premises than to present the request of the local preacher to the quarterly or district conference.

Section V.—*Exhorters.*

1. Exhorters were recognized in our Church at a very early period. Mr. Wesley permitted none of his members to hold religious meetings without a special note from the assistant.

2. The character of the office is sufficiently indicated by the name. It is not contemplated

that an exhorter will attempt to preach,—formally announce a text, and confine himself to the elucidation of any particular passage of Scripture,—but that he will read a Scripture lesson, and make a practical application of its general sentiments to the people. This office, when faithfully discharged, may be rendered eminently serviceable in promoting the interests of the Church.

3. It was required by the conference of 1779 that " every exhorter and local preacher should go by the directions of the assistants,—where, and only where, they shall appoint." They should act under the general direction of the preacher in charge. Exhorters and local preachers should co-operate with the traveling preachers in carrying out the general plan of the circuit; and should not hold meetings beyond the limits of the charge which recommended their license, unless they go forth to break up new ground, or are invited to another charge by the requisite authority of the Church.

4. No person can be licensed as an exhorter who is not a member in full connection, or who has not been first recommended by the leaders and stewards' meeting, or by the class of which

he is a member where no leaders' meeting is held.

5. All licenses to exhort are primarily given by the preacher in charge. Every exhorter, however, is subject to an annual examination of character in the district or quarterly conference; and his license must annually be renewed by the presiding elder, or the preacher in charge, if approved by the quarterly conference.

6. Exhorters are responsible for their official conduct to the district or quarterly conference; but they cannot be deprived of membership without a trial, in due form, before a committee of the society of which they are members.

CHAPTER IV.
CERTIFICATES AND LOVE-FEASTS.

Section I.—*Note of Recommendation.*

1. Every member in full connection, who removes to another circuit or station, is entitled to a note of recommendation, if charges are not preferred against him.

2. If, in the judgment of the preacher in charge, there are sufficient reasons for withholding a certificate, and the member is willing to be tried, the preacher is guilty of maladministration unless he proceeds in the trial of such person. (Discipline, ¶ 184, § 6.)

3. No preacher is under obligation to give a certificate of membership to any member of the Methodist Episcopal Church, unless said member wishes to remove his membership to another charge in the Methodist Episcopal Church; though, as a matter of courtesy, he may give a recommendation to a member in good standing

who wishes to unite with another evangelical denomination. (Discipline, ¶ 184, § 8.)

4. Where pastoral charges are contiguous, there may be a change of Church relation from the one to the other without a change of residence; but if the member removes his residence beyond the reach of his privileges, and the oversight of his pastor and leader, he should remove his membership by certificate, unless he has no access to Church privileges convenient to his new residence.

5. When a member receives a certificate of membership from a preacher having charge of a circuit or station, he is responsible for his moral conduct, from the date of his certificate until he joins, to the society which gave him that certificate. But in accordance with the action of the General Conference of 1884, a certificate of membership holds good for only one year, unless circumstances shall have made it impracticable for the holder to present it within the time limit. In such case, the certificate may be renewed by the preacher who gave it.

6. Certificates of removal must be signed by the preacher in charge, or if there be no

preacher in charge, by the presiding elder, and shall read as follows:

"*This certifies that A. B., the bearer, is an acceptable member of the .... Methodist Episcopal Church in ...., and is affectionately commended to the fellowship of the Methodist Episcopal Church in ...., or in any other Church to which he may present this certificate. When admitted to another charge, his relation to this charge will cease.*"

7. It is not optional with the preacher whether he will receive a certificate from a member residing within the limits of his charge, if presented within the prescribed time limit. If the certificate is drawn up in due form, and signed by the constituted authority, it must be honored, unless it is known that the person presenting the certificate has committed crime, in which case the Church issuing the certificate should immediately call the person to trial in due form before the society, or a select number of them.

The General Conference of 1860 made the following decision:

"Is a preacher in charge *obliged* to receive a properly authenticated certificate of a member when he is aware such reception would disturb the peace and quiet of the Church?

"*Ans.* It is the duty of the preacher to receive all such certificates."—*Gen. Conf. Jour.*, p. 298.

In those extreme special cases in which a preacher refuses to receive a letter, he must justify his course, if complained of, before the annual conference.

8. "When a member is expelled from the Church, and complaint is made against the administrator to his annual conference for maladministration, and the conference decide that the person was expelled contrary to Discipline, what is the relation of the member expelled from the Church? Does the act of the annual conference restore the character of the member, so that the charges on which he was expelled are so annulled that the preacher may legally give him a letter before said charges are disposed of by trial or withdrawn?

"*Ans.* The act of the annual conference does not restore his character, but simply his membership; and when so restored he is placed in the position which he occupied before he was tried, that is, he is an accused member, and hence the preacher is not at liberty to give him a certificate of membership."—*Gen. Conf. Jour.*, 1860, p. 298.

9. Neither a class-leader, nor any other Church officer, except the preacher of the circuit, can properly give a note of recommendation.

10. Certificates should not be given to those who withdraw from our Church, and do not intend to unite with any other evangelical Church.

11. Exhorters who change their residence should receive a note of recommendation, certifying their official relation; and the presiding elder having the oversight of the charge to which they have removed may direct that the names of such exhorters be entered upon the records of the district or quarterly conference.

12. To exercise a Christian watch-care over those who have removed among strangers, it is made the duty of the preacher in charge when he gives a letter to notify the pastor within whose bounds the persons having received such certificate shall have removed.. (Discipline, ¶ 184, § 6.)

SECTION II.—*Love-Feasts.*

1. Love-feasts, or *agapæ*, were instituted in the apostolic age. The early Christians ate and drank together to signify their Christian love for each other. Before receiving their repast they washed their hands, and public

prayers were offered. The services were conducted by the bishop, or presbyter. A portion of the sacred writings was read, and questions were proposed by the presiding officer respecting the lesson, which were answered by the assembly. Religious intelligence which had been received from other Churches was recited, and the acts of the martyrs, and letters from bishops and other eminent members of the Church, were read. Hymns and psalms were sung, and a collection was taken for the widow and the orphan, for the poor, the prisoner, and those who had suffered shipwreck.

These seasons were peculiarly interesting to the hated and hunted disciples, and rendered doubly dear because their religious professions cut them off from associations with their early friends. "It is a custom," says Chrysostom, "most beautiful and beneficial; for it is a supporter of love, a solace of poverty, a moderator of wealth, and a discipline of humility."

2. Many of the rites which a guiding Providence had made subservient to the interests of the Church in the days of her affliction began to be perverted when prosperity dawned upon her. Some hoped, by merely banqueting with the Church, to secure a moral qualification for

admission into the sacred mysteries; others supposed that by providing general *agapæ* for their brethren, they would perform a meritorious work which would personally exalt them in the sight of God and man; and others gave occasion for pagans to suspect that the same immoralities were practiced in the Christian festivals that disgraced their own. For these and other reasons the love-feasts were discontinued, in the Western Church, by order of the Council of Carthage, A.D. 397. (See Tertullian's Apol. i, 39; Apostol. Constitution, Book II, c. 28; Kitto's Sac. Lit., Art. *Agapæ*.)

3. Mr. Wesley assigns the following reasons for their introduction into the Methodistic economy: "In order to increase in them [persons in bands] a grateful sense of all his [God's] mercies, I desired that one evening in a quarter all the men in band, on a second all the women, would meet; and on a third both men and women together; that we might together 'eat bread,' as the ancient Christians did, 'with gladness and singleness of heart.' At these love-feasts (so we termed them, retaining the name as well as the thing, which was in use from the beginning) our food is only a little plain cake and water; but we seldom return

from them without being fed, not only with the 'meat which perisheth,' but with 'that which endureth to everlasting life.'"— *Wesley's Works*, vol. v, p. 183.

4. Members, probationers, and "well-disposed" baptized children of our members are entitled to admission into the love-feast of the circuit or station to which he belongs. (See Discipline, 1840.) The term "*strangers*" embraces all other persons, whether members of other Christian communions or not.

5. By established usage the presiding elder is entitled to hold the love-feast at the quarterly meeting.

CHAPTER V.
CHURCH TRIALS.

SECTION I.—*Trial of Members.*

1. WE now enter upon a subject of the greatest importance to the pastor. The pastoral office is instituted to guard and promote the moral and religious character of the community. In the discharge of its functions counsel, admonition, and reproof must frequently be administered, to establish the wavering and to reclaim the erring. It cannot be anticipated that those duties which call in question the rectitude of moral character can be discharged, with true Christian fidelity, without occasionally inflaming the bad passions of men, and, perhaps, subjecting one's self to a legal prosecution; and hence it is important to inquire how far the civil law recognizes the right of the full discharge of pastoral duties. Our political constitutions guarantee, in general terms, to every individual the natural and inalienable right to worship God according to the dictates of his own conscience, and promise that no subject shall be hurt, mo-

lested, or restrained, in person, liberty, or estate, for his religious sentiments or professions, provided that he does not disturb the public peace, nor infringe upon the rights of others. But these principles have been regarded as the basis of religious freedom, and the pledge that an enlightened conscience shall not be violated, rather than the foe to those religious associations which bind its members to watch over each other's faith and practice with a godly jealousy. It is not pretended that Churches in this country possess, in a legal aspect, more power than other societies voluntarily organized, with such gradations of officers and judicatories as may subserve the moral and religious purposes of their organization. No civil disabilities nor pecuniary fines can be inflicted for the grossest violations of covenant vows; yet the right of religious societies to inquire into the conduct of their members, to pass votes of expulsion, and record their proceedings against those who violate their covenant relations, has been fully recognized by the civil tribunal : nor will courts of justice inquire whether the conduct of the aggrieved member merited such discipline, provided that the proceedings of the Church were according to the established usages of the denomination, and done in good faith without malice. And even if the case has been submitted to a jury, on the trial of the indictment against the accused, and the evidence considered insufficient by them to convict the accused of the crime in question, it serves as no bar to the religious society investigating the case *de novo*, according to its established regulations. (Ref. 3 Johnson, 183.)

2. There are certain privileged communications which, although they may inflict real injury upon personal reputation, yet do not subject a person to a criminal prosecution, on the ground that the good of society required the divulging of private infamy. The giving of the character of a servant to a person about to employ him may be slanderous or otherwise, as it is done with honest intentions, or with a design to injure and defame. A representation made by members of a religious society to the pastor, or to a Church judicatory having power to hear, examine, and redress grievances, in respect to the ministry or laity, is *prima facie* a privileged communication. " The law concedes," says Judge Cowen, " the right of petition and remonstrance to a spiritual superior, when they are presented with a view to redress. The proper channel being pursued, the Church member is

entitled to the same measure of protection as if he had, when writing the libel, been engaged in seeking the removal of an inferior officer at the hands of a superior, created by the constitution or the law."—19 *Wendall*, 296 ; 23 *Wendall*, 26 ; 2 *Pick.*, 310.

3. It is a principle clearly recognized by the Discipline of our Church, that no member, in full connection, can be dropped or expelled by the preacher in charge until the select committee, or the society of which he is a member, declares, in due form, that he is guilty of the violation of some scriptural or moral principle, or some requisition of Church covenant. The restrictive rules guarantee, both to our ministers and members, the privilege of trial and of appeal ; and the General Conference has explicitly declared that " it is the right of every member of the Methodist Episcopal Church to remain in said Church, unless guilty of the violation of its rules ; and there exists no power in the ministry, either individually or collectively, to deprive any member of said right."—*Gen. Conf. Jour.*, 1848, p. 73. The fact that the member is guilty of the violation of the rules of the Church must be formally proved before the body holding original jurisdiction in the case.

If the administrator personally knows that the charges are substantially true, it does not authorize him to remove the accused member. The law recognizes no member as guilty until the evidence of guilt is duly presented to the proper tribunal, and the verdict is rendered.

4. The mode of removing unworthy members, in former times, was very different from the one now practiced. At every quarterly visitation Mr. Wesley gave a ticket to each member bearing the member's name upon it. This ticket was a symbol, or *tessera*, as the ancients termed such, denoting that the person holding it was recognized as a member of the society.

"These," says Mr. Wesley, "also supplied us with a quiet and inoffensive method of removing any disorderly member. He has no new ticket at the quarterly visitation—for so often the tickets are changed—and hereby it is immediately known that he is no longer of the community."—*Wesley's Works*, vol. v, p. 182.

SECTION II.—*President of the Trial.*

1. An accused member must be brought to trial before a committee in the presence of the preacher in charge, who shall preside in the

trial. The Discipline requires that the preacher in charge shall pronounce him expelled whom the select committee have found guilty of a crime expressly forbidden in the word of God. If members willfully and habitually neglect the means of grace (Discipline, ¶ 234) and will not amend, it is made the duty of "*him who has the charge of the circuit or station* to bring their case before the society, or a select number of them." The preacher in charge is required to "receive, *try*, and *expel* members, according to the form of Discipline." The history of the rule confirms the exposition we have given. The section respecting "bringing to trial disorderly members" was drawn up by Bishop Asbury, in 1788, and introduced into the Discipline in the following year. The original section did not specify by whom the convicted member should be expelled, but it was indefinitely stated, "Let him be expelled." But a note was appended to the Minutes, in the same year, explanatory of this section, and setting forth upon whom the responsibility of conducting a Church trial rested: "As a very few persons have in some respects mistaken our meaning, in the thirty-second section of our form of Discipline, on bringing to trial disorderly members, etc., we think it necessary to explain it. When a member of our society is to be tried for any offense, the *officiating minister*, or *preacher*, is to call together all the members, if the society be small, or a select number of it if it be large, to take knowledge, and give advice, and bear witness to the justice of the whole process; that improper and private expulsions may be prevented for the future." In 1792 the rule was amended, to remove all obscurity, so as to read: "Let the minister or preacher *who has the charge of the circuit* expel him." Rev. William Watters, the first American preacher who joined the itinerancy, also shows how the rule was understood in the days of the fathers. "But while he [the bishop] superintends the whole work," he remarks, "he cannot interfere with the particular charge of any of the preachers in their stations. To see that the preachers fill their places with propriety, and to understand the state of every station or circuit, that he may the better make the appointment of the preachers, is, no doubt, no small part of his duty; but he has nothing to do with *receiving, censuring,* or *excluding* members: *this belongs wholly to the stationed preacher* and *members*."—*Memoirs*, p. 105.

2. A presiding elder may appoint a preacher from another circuit on his district to the charge,

to preside at a Church trial, when the circumstances of the case seem to demand it. In such cases the former preacher in charge becomes a junior preacher, until the close of the trial. But no preacher in charge can transfer his authority to another preacher on his own responsibility.

3. A junior preacher cannot preside at the trial of a member. If the senior preacher cannot attend, the presiding elder should put the junior preacher, or some other preacher, in charge during the trial.

4. "In all trials of members or preachers, whether by committee or before a conference, and in all appeals, it is improper for the presiding officer at the trial to deliver a charge to the committee [or conference] explaining the evidence and setting forth the merits of the case."—*Discipline*, ¶ 246.

SECTION III.—*Complaint.*

1. When public rumor accuses a member of having committed a crime, prudential considerations would dictate that the pastor, or a committee, be appointed to visit the person so

accused, and examine the foundation of the reports, before any other action is taken. If the reports are evidently unfounded, the member is not mortified by the additional report that he has been arraigned before the Church. Such a committee is prepared also to rescue the character of a suffering brother, by a presentation of the facts which a diligent investigation elicited. Such a procedure also shows the care and jealousy with which the Church watches over the Christian reputation of her members.

2. The administrator of discipline must ordinarily reduce to suitable form the charges and specifications from the rough story of the complainant. To give no attention to any complaints except such as are presented in due form, is to neglect the greatest number of those requiring the special investigation of the Church.

3. A bill of charges should not be drawn on the mere declaration of a complainant that he " has probable cause to suspect " a member of being guilty of crime; but even this, under some circumstances, might justify the raising of a committee to investigate the facts in the case. Nor is a report, made by one whose testimony

would not be received in an ecclesiastical court, a sufficient basis to justify an arrest of character, unless there are collateral circumstances or facts to corroborate the statements of the accuser.

4. Any crime, committed at however remote a period, if it be within the time in which the accused has been a member of the Church, is indictable; but it cannot extend to any period beyond membership. Charges of immorality against preachers should not be restricted to the time in which they have been in the ministry, but may extend to any time within their Church membership.

5. It does not destroy the actionable character of a complaint, that the predecessor of the administrator, though acquainted with the facts, took no legal notice of them. The indictable character of an act depends upon the fact whether it is a violation of the moral law and Church covenant, and not upon the administration of frail man.

6. Accessories to crime may be complained of before or after the fact; and the same proceedings should be had, in every respect, as if

the accused were charged of being principal in the offense.

7. In drawing out a bill of charges the following order should be observed:
 a. A brief statement of the charge.
 b. The specification, or specifications, by which it is sustained.

This order should be observed until every charge is presented, and the different specifications are arranged under their appropriate heads. For example:
 I. Charge—Theft.
  1. Specification—"In taking, on the fourth of July," etc.
  2. Specification— ———.
 II. Charge—Falsehood.
  1. Specification—"In saying," etc.
  2. Specification— ———.

8. The object of the rule requiring the charge to be particularly set forth is threefold: first, to apprise the accused of the precise nature of the charge made against him; secondly, to enable the court to determine whether the facts constitute an offense, and to render the proper award thereon; and, thirdly, that the judgment may be a bar to any future prose-

cution for the same offense. (3 Stark. Ev., 1527.)

9. Every charge should involve an offense which, if fully sustained, and without any mitigating circumstances, would be of a sufficiently aggravating character to demand a special Church penalty.

10. There should be a perfect correspondence between the charge and the specifications. Every specification, if fully sustained, ought to be of such a character as to sustain the charge; and it ought not to involve a higher or a lower offence than that which is charged in the bill. If the charge is immorality, no specifications should be given under it which involve only an imprudence; and if the charge is imprudent conduct, no specification should be given which involves an immorality.

11. Every charge should be expressed in as mild language as possible, and yet involve an actionable offence; and as few charges and specifications should be given as practicable, and yet secure the great object of Church action.

12. Two distinct crimes should not be set forth under one charge, unless they are of such a character that, when they are committed, they constitute but one legal offence—as assault and battery: the latter includes the former. And each specification should set forth one, and only one, averment of the offence specified in the charge. The specifications should be stated in the most explicit and perspicuous language, and all immaterial facts, not necessary ingredients of the offence, should be carefully avoided. All averments should be made positively that the accused did so and so, and not by way of recital or argument.

13. Every complaint, setting forth a crime, should specify, as far as possible, the time and place in which it was committed; but the charge of disseminating erroneous doctrine, or of being unacceptable, inefficient, or secular, does not, in most cases, admit of specific particularity. In these cases, it is the serial character of the acts which, to a very great extent, constitutes the offence.

14. Any error in the name of the person, or in the circumstances described in the bill of charges, provided the general meaning is clearly

expressed, and the error is of such a character as not to change the issue of the case, ought not to be deemed a bar to the proceedings. The ends of justice ought never to suffer from mere technicalities; but the charges and specifications must be so correctly drawn that the accused may fully understand, from the complaint itself, the true nature of the case, and what he must show to establish his innocence.

15. All complaints setting forth charges and specifications must be signed by some member of the Church. If the complaint is originally made by a person not a member of the Church, the bill of charges must be signed by one over whom the Church exercises jurisdiction. It is not necessary that the person signing the bill of charges should be an *accuser*, in the sense of the Discipline. "An *aggrieved* person," says Bishop M'Kendree, "may be a *complainant;* but our Discipline does not recognize any one as an *accuser* unless he be a witness in the case against the accused."

16. It is not advisable that a presiding elder should sign a bill of charges against a preacher which must be investigated before himself; nor should a preacher in charge sign a bill of charges

against one of his members, unless the members of the Church refuse to do it. In those cases where a preacher in charge feels it his duty to prefer a charge against a member of his flock, the presiding elder should, ordinarily, put some other preacher in charge to try the case.

It is a principle universally regarded in civil proceedings that no judge shall be counsel, nor act as attorney, nor advise nor assist any party in any case which will come before him; and the principle is so manifestly founded in justice that it should not be disregarded in ecclesiastical proceedings. In those extreme cases where a member cannot be found who will sign a bill of charges, there must exist such peculiarities and difficulties in the case as not only to require a strictly impartial presiding officer, but one who will have the reputation of being impartial.

17. Where several persons are accused of having been connected in the commission of any crime, the charges and specifications should be made out separately, and each person tried separately.

18. Every member accused of crime is entitled to a copy of the charges and specifications, for

a time sufficiently long before the trial for him to prepare his defense.

19. If a copy of the charges and specifications, duly signed, is left at the usual residence of the accused, it should be deemed a sufficient citation, even if the accused has fled from the place, or his present residence is not known.

SECTION IV.—*Select Committee.*

1. The Discipline requires that an accused member shall be brought " before a committee of not less than five, (except in case of neglect of duty, in which case the accused may be brought before the society or a select committee,) who shall not be members of the quarterly conference; and if the preacher judge necessary, the committee may be selected from any part of the district." In either case it should be understood that only members in full connection are intended. In 1789 the following explanation of the rule was published in the Discipline : " The officiating minister or preacher is to call together all the members, if the society be small, or a select number if it be large."

2. If the accused member is brought before a select number, the preacher in charge must ap-

point them. And "in case of trial before a select committee, the parties may challenge for cause." (Discipline, ¶ 230.)

3. "In selecting a committee for the trial of a member," Bishop Hedding remarks, "a preacher ought to be very careful to obtain wise, pious, and candid men, who will do justice both to the accused person and to the Church. There should be a sufficient number of them to form a respectable court: for the decision of so important a matter should not be left to two or three individuals."

The committee should consist of men of such acknowledged virtue and integrity that their opinions will be respected both by the Church and the world. Many persons of deep and ardent piety, unaccustomed to weigh evidence and balance testimony, and whose hearts are full of gushing sympathy for the erring, are not well qualified to discharge the duties of a select committee, where the honor and reputation of the Church are at stake. No less qualifications, certainly, should be deemed satisfactory in those who sit in solemn judgment on the moral and Christian reputation of one for whom Christ died, than is demanded of the juror at a civil tribunal. Such are required to be men of probity and intelligence, free from personal interest and party prejudice: much more should the Christian man be free from all undue bias while investigating the character of a professed member of the body of Christ. The peace and prosperity of the Church, and the salvation of the accused, stand so closely connected with the results of a Church trial, that justice and equity should be most impartially administered. Many causes, such as kindred, prejudice, etc., which would not render one incompetent as a witness, are sufficient to disqualify him as a member of the select committee. The committee must not be composed of members of the quarterly conference; that, in case of appeal, a new tribunal may decide upon the merits of the case. (Discipline, ¶ 230.)

4. "The circumstances of the case," says Chief-Justice Pennington, "the probable or improbable nature of the facts detailed, the character of the witness, the manner of his giving testimony, must all be taken into consideration, and ought, after being duly weighed, to carry conviction to the minds of the jury before they give it [the testimony] an effect by their verdict. Should a witness relate a fact which, from its improbable nature, or from the badness of the character of the witness, taken together with the

circumstances in the case, on due consideration does not carry a belief of the fact home to the minds of the jury, but, on the other hand, they believe what the witness hath related is false,— in that case what he has said is no evidence to them, and they are not bound to give any weight to it; but, on the contrary, if they act upon it, or rather make up their verdict upon it, such conduct is a departure from their duty, and little short of a violation of their oath." The weight of testimony is a question belonging to the select committee exclusively.

5. The committee have no right, in forming their opinion, to take into consideration any facts within their own cognizance, of which no evidence was presented in the trial. If any member of the committee knew any important fact, he should have stated it as a witness.

6. Making up judgment.
a. The committee should first inquire whether the specifications have been sustained by evidence.
b. Whether, the specifications being sustained, the charge is proved. All the specifications may be proved, and yet the charge be not sustained; but if the specifications are not sus-

tained, the charge, of course, cannot be sustained in the highest degree.

c. The whole question of guilt rests upon the decision of the committee. It is to decide, if the charge is one of immorality, whether the crime is one of the first or second degree. There may be palliating circumstances which should be taken into the account, and which greatly modify the guilt, and hence should change the penalty. Bishop Hedding remarks: "Another question has arisen here. When the 'select number' judges a member guilty of the *act* of which he is accused, who is to judge whether that *act* is a crime, in the sense of the rule—the select number or the preacher? The select number: for the crime is included in the judgment of 'guilty.' When the judgment of guilty is rendered, the rule says, 'Let the preacher in charge expel him.'"

d. The judgment of the committee should never be given VERBALLY, but should be *written*, and *signed* by all of the committee who approve of the decision. A majority of the committee is competent to render a verdict in a Church trial.

It is not expected of the committee that it will set forth, in its verdict, the grounds of its judgment; but there may be circumstances in which this may be necessary.

The committee is allowed to have before it all the maps, charts, and written documents which were admitted during the trial.

7. The question has frequently been asked, May the preacher remain with the select number while they are making up their judgment? In reply, Bishop Hedding remarks: "Certainly he ought, for he is pastor of the flock; and he would greatly neglect his duty were he to be absent, and consequently not know on what law or evidence the judgment is rendered." Mr. Wesley believed that the New Testament makes the pastor responsible to Christ for the purity of the flock, and hence he should judge as to the guilt or innocence of the accused member. Our fathers administered the Discipline on this principle up to the year 1800. It was then provided that the society, or select committee, should pronounce an opinion upon the guilt or innocence of the accused; and the action of the preacher was to be governed by this decision. The entire responsibility of the decision, we repeat, rests alone upon the committee. The preacher, under no circumstances, should attempt to balance the evidence, weigh probabilities, determine the credibility of witnesses, or draw inferences from the facts proved, and thus

determine disputed questions of fact, even at the request of the parties. "No judicious administrator of the Discipline," says Bishop Morris, "will let the committee, or any other person, know his opinion of the case, either before the trial or during its progress, till the members of the committee have made their decision and signed their names to it."

8. When the words of a charge or specification are susceptible of two meanings, the select committee must determine in what sense they are used.

9. When an accused member is brought to trial before the society, all members in full connection, whether males or females, are entitled to vote. The select committee may consist in part of females, where the circumstances seem to demand it. Usage, however, restricts the select committee to males. (Bishop Janes.)

SECTION V.—*The Trial.*

1. It is the duty of the presiding officer to conduct the religious services of the occasion, to read the names of the select committee and the counsel of the parties, to appoint a secretary to

keep a correct record of the trial, to read the charges and specifications to the accused, to decide who are competent witnesses, and whether the documents offered are admissible, and to decide all questions of law which arise in the process of the trial. If the accused is expelled, and dissatisfied with the ruling of the presiding officer, he has the following remedy: on a question of law, either party may appeal to the decision of the president of the next annual conference; on dissatisfaction, the accused may appeal to the ensuing quarterly conference, or he may charge the presiding officer with maladministration before the annual conference.

2. Mode of conducting a trial.
a. The arraignment.
   (1.) Reading the charges and specifications to the accused.
   (2.) Demanding his reply to the charge.
b. The accuser calls and examines his witnesses. Cross-examination by the accused.
c The accused puts in his evidence. Cross-examination by the accuser.
d. Rebutting testimony by the accuser.
e. Rebutting testimony by the accused.
f. Closing arguments.
   (1.) By the accuser.

(2.) By the accused.
(3.) By the accuser.
g. Verdict by the committee.
h. Announcement of acquittal or expulsion by the presiding officer.

3. If the accused voluntarily confesses that he is guilty of the charge, no further evidence will of course follow : the case is at once to be submitted to the committee.

4. If the accused refuses to answer to the charge, or answers foreign to the purpose, it is deemed in law equivalent to answering not guilty, unless he is dumb *ex visitatione Dei.*

5. No member can be held to answer on a second indictment for any offense of which he has been acquitted by a committee, on the facts and merits, on a former trial. But if he is acquitted upon the ground of a variance between the indictment and the proof, or upon any exception to the form and substance of the indictment, he may be tried on a new process, and convicted for the same offense, notwithstanding such former acquittal. A plea of former acquittal is valid only when the accused has been acquitted in due form by a tribunal competent

to make a final disposition of the case. If a local or traveling preacher, therefore, should be acquitted by a committee called by the preacher in charge, or the presiding elder, such acquittal would serve as no bar to a subsequent arraignment, on the same charges and specifications, before the quarterly or district conference, or before the annual conference, as the case may be; for these tribunals alone have original jurisdiction over local and traveling preachers.

6. "May a person who has not been formally received into full connection in the Church, but has for a term of years enjoyed all the privileges of a member, and is supposed by the preacher in charge and society to be a member, plead the fact of his non-reception as a bar to proceedings in case of alleged immorality?

"*Ans.* No."—*Gen. Conf. Jour.*, 1860, p. 298.

7. When the accused has any special matter to plead in abatement, or bar to the proceedings, he should present it at the opening of the case.

8. Omissions and errors, when the true intent evidently appears, may be corrected; but no amendment can, during the progress of the trial, be admitted which in any degree changes

the issue of the case. During the trial a new charge or specification cannot be admitted; yet a charge or specification may be withdrawn before a verdict is rendered. For example, when a charge is brought for slander, consisting of two counts, say of theft and perjury, the specification of perjury may be withdrawn, and all the testimony by which it was supported, and the verdict be rendered merely in reference to the specification of theft.

9. When charges are preferred against a member, the preacher in charge has no right to rule out of the bill of charges any specification which is legally actionable under our rules of discipline; but an annual, district, or quarterly conference may retain or dismiss the whole or any part of the bill of charges, as it may judge proper.

10. When an important witness is absent by no fault of the party for which he is to testify, or when a party is surprised by evidence which he did not anticipate, the trial may be adjourned upon application of the party, at the discretion of the presiding officer, to some suitable time when all the important witnesses may be present.

11. Averments of immaterial facts, not necessary ingredients in the offense, and without which the complaint would be good, may be rejected, and need not be proved.

12. If an accused member evades a trial by absenting himself after sufficient notice has been given, and without requesting any one to appear in his behalf, it does not preclude the necessity of a formal trial. The preacher in charge should appoint competent counsel to conduct the defense, and all the evidence in the case should be presented in due form to the committee. If the committee decide that the circumstances of the accusation afford strong presumption of guilt, the accused is to be esteemed as guilty, and accordingly excluded by the preacher in charge; but in no case can expulsion take place until such a verdict is rendered. The committee, and not the preacher in charge, must decide when a member "evades a trial," in the sense of the Discipline.

13. The trial must be limited to the particular charge brought against the accused. If a different crime is proved from the one alleged against him, he cannot be held to answer to it, unless there is a new bill of charges, setting

forth the particular offense complained of, and a trial *de novo* held, according to the form of Discipline.

·14. There may be circumstances which would justify a preacher in refusing to entertain a bill of charges, even when signed by respectable members of the Church. In such cases the accusers may, if they deem it proper, complain of the preacher to his presiding elder, or to the conference, for neglect of duty; and the presiding elder may remove him from the charge, and the conference try him for neglect of ministerial duty.

15. After charges have been entertained, and the trial has proceeded until the complainant has produced his testimony, the case cannot then be dismissed without the consent of the complainant. (Bishop Waugh.)

16. If the accused desires assistance in conducting his defense, all necessary aid should be given him, and he should be allowed to make full defense by himself and counsel, and to make any proof by competent witnesses whom he may produce. The accused member may select his own counsel, provided that such coun-

sel is a member in good and regular standing in the Methodist Episcopal Church.

17. It is highly improper, ordinarily, to conduct a trial in a public congregation. None should be present except the parties summoned; at least, unless they are members of the Church.

18. When testimony has been admitted and journalized, it cannot be taken from the record without the consent of both parties.

19. "In all cases of trial and appeal it is improper for the presiding officer to deliver a charge to the committee explaining the evidence and setting forth the merits of the case."—*Discipline*, ¶ 246.

SECTION VI.—*General Laws of Evidence.*

1. Every administrator of Discipline should have a correct knowledge of the general laws of evidence, as established by the civil judiciary; for though in ecclesiastical courts mere technicalities should never subvert the principles of equity, yet the general laws of evidence established by the wisdom of ages are as applicable in establishing matters of fact before an

ecclesiastical tribunal as before a civil. Some of these principles are the following :

2. First. The evidence must correspond with the allegations, and be confined to the point in issue. It is supposed that nothing will be expressed in the bill of charges which is immaterial; and hence every allegation set forth should be supported by direct testimony. If, however, the specifications are drawn out with unnecessary particularity, a judicious committee might consider as surplusage whatever is not necessary to constitute the crime. Extraneous facts tend to draw away the minds of the committee from the point in issue, and operate unjustly upon the accused; for he cannot be supposed to have prepared himself to meet any point except the general one set forth in the bill of charges.

3. Secondly. It is sufficient if the substance of the issue be proved. The civil law makes a distinction between allegations of matter of substance and allegations of essential description. It is sufficient if the former be substantially proved; but the latter must be proved with literal precision. In ecclesiastical trials, where we have to deal with actions which are criminal in themselves, whatever may have been the

circumstances in which they took place, the rule may be applied, with hardly an exception, that it is sufficient if the substance of the allegation be proved. "If, in an action for malicious prosecution, the plaintiff alleges that he was acquitted of the charge on a certain day, here the substance of the allegation is the acquittal; and it is sufficient if this fact be proved on any day, the time not being material." If the averment is divisible, and enough is proved to constitute an offense, it would be deemed sufficient, both in a civil and in an ecclesiastical court, that one part merely was proved. Thus an indictment for stealing two notes of equal value would be sustained if the evidence only proved that one note was stolen. In a proceeding to protect public morals, nothing should be deemed essential but that which constitutes the act of crime.

4. Thirdly. The obligation of proving any fact lies upon the party who substantially asserts the affirmative of the issue. It is generally sufficient to oppose a direct denial to a direct allegation, until it is established by evidence, or by strong collateral circumstances. As the party in the affirmative is entitled to begin and to reply, he should bring forward all his evi-

dence before any defense is made. The rule seems to have been based upon the fact that, in most cases, it is impossible to prove a negative as readily and explicitly as an affirmative. If a man has indulged in the use of ardent spirits to intoxication, that is usually susceptible of proof; but it might be exceedingly difficult for an innocent man to prove that he was not intoxicated on a given day.

5. Fourthly. The best evidence should be procured of which the nature of the case is susceptible. This rule does not forbid the introduction of testimony of different degrees of strength, but it requires that strong evidence should not be withheld when it is known to be in the possession of the party. When such testimony is withheld, the design is evidently fraudulent. Oral testimony cannot be substituted for documentary, when such testimony can be procured.

6. Hearsay evidence. This term is applied both to written and to oral testimony, and relates to such as does not derive its value solely from the credit given to the witness himself, but rests also, in part, on the veracity of others. Hearsay evidence is universally held as incom-

petent to establish any specific fact which is susceptible of being proved by living witnesses. "If," says Justice Buller, "the first speech were without oath, another oath that there was such speech makes it no more than a bare speaking, and so of no value in a court of justice."—*Bull. N. P.*, 294.

7. In the following cases hearsay testimony is received in civil courts:

a. In matters of public and general interest, where the health or happiness, reputation or prosperity, of the whole community is involved.

b. In matters of ancient possessions, where it is supposed that no original witnesses are now living.

c. Declarations and entries made by persons since deceased, and against the interests of the persons making them at the time they were made.

d. Dying declarations of sane persons.

e. The testimony of deceased witnesses, given in a former action between the same parties.

SECTION VII.—*Witnesses.*

1. The Roman law required the evidence of two witnesses as the foundation of a decree. In our courts one witness, if his testimony is cor-

roborated by strong collateral circumstances, is sufficient to establish facts. In ecclesiastical trials, while a single allegation, rebutted by a positive denial, should not be deemed sufficient to destroy the Christian character of one in whom the Church had reposed the fullest confidence, yet a single testimony, corroborated by strong collateral circumstances, may convince an intelligent committee of the moral certainty of the guilt of the accused.

2. Common law forbids that a party to the record in a civil suit should testify, either for himself or for a co-suitor in the case; and the same principle holds equally good in all ecclesiastical examinations. Nevertheless, in many of the States *statutes* have been enacted, allowing parties in civil suits, and even those charged with having committed the highest crimes, to testify in the case, the tribunal of course giving such weight to the testimony as may seem proper under all the circumstances. If the complainant has no other interest in the case than is common to all the members of the Church, he should be allowed to testify.

3. Neither husband nor wife can testify in any civil or criminal cause in which one of them

is a party. To secure domestic happiness, it is held that neither of them should be required to divulge any confidential communications obtained by the hallowed confidence of the marriage relation. No other relationship, except that of husband and wife, disqualifies a person from testifying for or against another. In ecclesiastical courts, however, the husband and wife should mutually be allowed to testify for each other, and the committee should give such weight to their testimony as they consider it is entitled to.

4. Persons deficient in understanding are incompetent witnesses.

When the deaf and dumb are produced in civil courts, it must be shown by the party producing them that they are persons of sufficient understanding to give testimony.

In regard to children, there is no precise age within which they are absolutely rejected. At the age of fourteen it is presumed that every person is competent, until the opposite is shown. Some have been admitted as early as five years of age to testify in civil courts.

5. Persons insensible to the obligations of an oath, as atheists, and those made infamous by

having been convicted of flagrant crimes, as felony, forgery, perjury, etc., are deemed incompetent to testify before a civil tribunal. Nor should they be listened to in an ecclesiastical investigation, unless their statements are corroborated by strong collateral circumstances, or they have been reformed in their morals.

6. Persons of reputed veracity are competent witnesses in a Church trial, without regard to their particular religious belief or Church relation. "Witnesses from without" the pale of the Church "shall not be rejected."

7. The presiding officer of a trial must determine the competency of a witness; but the society, or select committee, must determine what weight, if any, should be given to the testimony.

8. Though we would not say that a pastor is not a competent witness against any of his flock, yet we would repeat, that if he is the principal witness, the presiding elder should put another preacher in charge to preside at the trial. In civil courts the same person cannot be both judge and witness. If another judge is present and presides, a judge may be sworn and testify;

but not otherwise. And though a preacher in charge does not sustain the same relation to an ecclesiastical court that a judge does to a civil, yet there are so many analogies between them that it is ordinarily inexpedient that the same person should be both presiding officer of the trial and a witness.

SECTION VIII.—*Examination of Witnesses.*

1. Witnesses are to be examined first by the party producing them, and afterward cross-examined by the opposite party.

2. The presiding officer may order that the witnesses be examined out of the hearing of each other, when he deems it essential to the discovery of truth.

3. Each witness should be called upon to relate what he knows of the case, and his testimony should be written, and to insure perfect accuracy in the records, read to him as taken by the secretary. Every question and answer should be written which either party deems essential to the case.

4. Leading questions are not allowed in direct examination, but they are admissible in cross-

examination. Leading questions are those which suggest to the witness the desired answer. Example: *Was not the said A——— B——— in M——— on the fourth of July last?* Leading questions are permitted in direct examination where the witness appears to be hostile to the party producing him, and where an omission is evidently caused by want of recollection.

5. A witness is not permitted to write down his testimony to read in court; but he is permitted to assist his memory by a written instrument or memorandum. It is not necessary that this memorandum should have been made by the witness, or be admissible in itself as evidence.

6. Witnesses in general must depose to such facts only as are within their own knowledge. In some cases persons are required to state their opinions or belief. Examples: the testimony of medical men, whether death could be produced by certain causes; whether certain circumstances indicated a sane or insane state of mind; the testimony of skillful penmen, whether a given writing were the veritable chirography of a particular person. Professional books are not admissible in evidence.

7. A witness, while giving his testimony, may recall and correct his testimony; but it should be taken down just as it is given, with all its corrections: and it is for the committee to decide whether the latter statements are more worthy of belief than the former.

8. All exceptions to evidence ought to be made at the time when it is first taken. After the verdict it is too late to take an exception.

9. Witnesses in civil courts are not compelled to answer any questions which will degrade or expose them to penal liability; but as our ecclesiastical courts are not so legalized that the witness is compelled to answer any question, this subject need not be considered. The presiding officer must decide whether the question is a proper one.

10. If no counsel appear for the complainant, the presiding officer should put such questions as may be necessary to elicit the truth, guarding carefully against any bias toward either party. No question should be put to a witness the relevancy of which does not appear.

11. A witness in an ecclesiastical court ought not to be put on oath: it can accomplish no

good. Such oaths are extrajudicial, and not legally binding. No oaths are held by the civil law to be obligatory except those given in some proceeding which the civil law recognizes. To swear falsely before a court incompetent to administer an oath is not perjury. (2 Caines, 91.)

12. Evidence of good character is inadmissible when the general character for veracity has not been impeached, even if an attempt is made to prove facts inconsistent with the statements of the witness.

13. A witness may be impeached in two ways:
a. By disproving the facts stated by him by the testimony of other witnesses.
b. By general evidence affecting his credit for veracity.

"In impeaching the character of a witness, [not a member of our Church,] it is not allowable to impeach his *general moral character*, but his general character *for veracity*, and that not by producing testimony of particular facts of bad moral conduct, but by producing testimony as to the general fact of his unreliability as a person of veracity."—*Gen. Conf. Jour.*, 1860, p. 428.

The general character of a member of our Church for veracity cannot be impeached; but the facts stated by him may be disproved by the testimony of other witnesses.

Section IX.—*Depositions.*

1. It is advisable, in all cases where it can be done, to produce all material witnesses at the trial. But as no ecclesiastical judicatory can compel the presence of any witness, it frequently becomes necessary to take depositions.

2. " The testimony of an absent witness may be taken before the preacher in charge, or a preacher appointed by the presiding elder of the district within which such witness resides; provided, in every case, sufficient notice has been given to the adverse party of the time and place of taking such testimony."—*Discipline,* ¶ 241. The notice should state the hour and place of taking the testimony, and be delivered to the party in person, or left at his usual place of residence. A notice left at a post-office is not sufficient, if it was not received by the party. What time is a reasonable notice to the adverse party in taking depositions is not fixed by the Discipline, but is a question of law which the

presiding officer must decide; ordinarily a week, at least, should be allowed

3. Form of notice:
To A. B. Whereas C. D. has requested me to take the deposition of E. F., of G., to be used in the examination of the charges and specifications preferred against you by C. D., I do, therefore, appoint the second day of June, 18—, at one o'clock P. M., at the house of the said E. F., as the time and place for the said person to testify what he knows relative to matters contained in the said charges and specifications. And you are hereby notified, that you may then and there be present, and put such interrogatories as you may judge fit.

Yours, etc., H. K., *Pastor*.

L——, *May* 20, 18—.

4. Form of deposition:
I, E. F., of G., testify and say that ——.

After the direct testimony of the deponent is written, the party taking the deposition is allowed, first, to examine him on all the points which he deems material; and then the adverse party may examine him in the same way. After which either party may propose such other interrogatories as the case may require.

If the accused objects to the admission of the person to testify in the case, this should be written down, stating the nature of the objection.

If any question is objected to by either party, as being leading, or irrelevant, or hearsay, or relating to matters of opinion, this should be noted under the question, and previous to the writing of the answer.

Ordinarily, great latitude should be allowed to the questions, if desired by either party; nor is it advisable, usually, at this stage of the proceedings, to decide on the validity of the objections, unless in very clear cases.

After the deposition is written, it should be read to the deponent, and signed by him. A note should be appended to every deposition, stating the reason of its being taken, and whether the adverse party was duly notified and attended.

5. Depositions should be sealed up by the person taking them, and remain sealed until opened by the proper authorities.

6. Depositions should be rejected if it appear that the opposite party was not notified to attend at the time and place appointed for taking

the deposition, or that a sufficient notice was not given, or that he was notified to attend at a time when he must necessarily be absent, or engaged in important business requiring his personal attention, and that this was known to the party giving the notice.

7. When witnesses are present at the seat of the conference, but refuse to give evidence in open conference, the conference has a right to appoint a commission to take their testimony, the opposite party being notified to appear before such commission, and having the right to cross-examine the witnesses. In such cases the testimony is to be taken by a secretary appointed by the commission; and, when reported to the conference, it must be filed and carefully preserved by the secretary of that body.

8. When only a part of a deposition is desired to be used in a trial, the whole of it must be read.

Section X.—*Appeal.*

1. The privilege of appeal is allowed both to preachers and members by the constitution of our Church, under certain limitations. The

General Conference "shall not do away the privileges of our ministers and preachers or trial by a committee, and of an appeal: neither shall they do away the privileges of our members of trial before the society, or by a committee, and of an appeal." It is required, however, in order that the appeal may be entertained, that the condemned person signify his intention to appeal within a given time.

2. The court appealed to, and not the court appealed from, is to judge whether or not the party has a right to appeal. As the right of appeal is not treated in the Restrictive Rules as a conditional one to be regulated by express enactments, great license should be given to this right. No appeal should be rejected unless there are very manifest reasons for it. It has never been considered, however, that the appellate court can exercise no discretion in any case of appeal,—that it must entertain every appeal that is made to it.

3. If an accused person evades a trial by absenting himself after sufficient notice has been given him, and the committee judge that the circumstances of the accusation afford strong presumption of guilt, he may be esteemed as

guilty, and be accordingly excluded. And a person who absents himself from trial can claim no right to an appeal. But mere absence from the place of trial does not show that the accused person evaded a trial by absenting himself, in the sense of the Discipline. He should be allowed to show to the quarterly conference that his absence from the trial was not designed, nor a fault on his part. If a majority of the quarterly conference are convinced that he did not designedly evade a trial, the appeal should be entertained.

4. "When a member of an annual conference gives notice to the conference that he has withdrawn from the Church or conference, and at the same time there be *charges* ready to be presented against him, and he has knowledge of such *charges* previous to his notice of withdrawal, and he has been marked upon the journal of the annual conference as withdrawn under *charges*, has such member the right to appeal to the General [now Judicial] Conference from such record of the annual conference?

"*Answer.* He has not."—*Gen. Conf. Jour.*, 1860, p. 298.

5. No appeal of an excluded member can be entertained, unless it is brought before the *next*

ensuing quarterly conference; or of a local preacher, unless he signify to the district or quarterly conference, as the case may be, his determination to appeal to the *next* annual conference; or of a traveling preacher, unless he signify his intention to appeal to the judicial conference at the time of his condemnation, or at any subsequent time when he is informed of it. The General Conference of 1860 adopted the following decision:

"When an expelled member has, by neglect or otherwise, forfeited his *right* of appeal, may a subsequent quarterly conference, if it desire to do so, grant him the *privilege* of an appeal?

"*Answer*. No."—*Gen. Conf. Jour.*, p. 298.

6. No district or quarterly conference can try an appeal when the testimony is not duly recorded. When accurate minutes have not been taken in the trial before the society, or a select number, "the case," says Bishop Hedding, "should be referred back for a new trial, that those who did their work carelessly, at first, may have opportunity of doing it properly, and of being admonished to avoid such errors afterward."

7. In case a local preacher appeals to the annual conference, and it is found that the

minutes of the trial were not signed by the president of the conference by which he was tried, and by a majority of the members of the conference who were present, the appeal cannot be entertained. When the Discipline has been illegally administered, the case should be remanded to the tribunal holding original jurisdiction over the member, for a new trial. (Bishop Soule.)

8. Mode of conducting appeals in the General [now Judicial] Conference.

(1.) Present the appeal.

(2.) Determine what members of the Committee on Appeals, not less than thirteen, shall hear and try the case—a majority of whom shall decide.

(3.) Read the findings in the case.

(4.) State the grounds of the appeal.

(5.) Motion to admit the appeal.

(6.) Read the minutes and documents.

(7.) Appellant's defense.

(8.) Reply of the delegates of the conference from whose action the appeal is taken.

(9.) Appellant's reply to the delegates.

(10.) Decision of the case.

9. The motion to admit the appeal is put to the court, that if the appellant is not entitled to

an appeal the facts of the case may be presented. In the following cases appeals may not be entertained :

a. When the accused absents himself from trial in a strictly disciplinary sense. (Discipline, ¶ 251.)

b. When he does not signify his intention to appeal within the specified time. (Discipline, ¶ 232, 257, 258. Gen. Conf. Jour., 1860, p. 298.)

c. When no censure or reproof was administered as a penalty, and the conference passed the character of the appellant without censure, and simply declared that he erred in judgment in the administration of Discipline. (Gen. Conf. Jour., 1840, pp. 82, 83.)

d. When the appellant declares himself withdrawn from the Church subsequent to the adjudication of his case and the avowal of his intention to appeal. (Gen. Conf. Jour., 1848, p. 38.)

e. If a member of an annual conference gives notice to the conference that he has withdrawn from the Church or conference, and at the same time there are charges ready to be preferred against him, and he has knowledge of such charges previous to his notice of withdrawal, if the conference should enter upon its journal that he withdrew under charges, he could claim no right to appeal from such record to the judicial conference. (Gen. Conf. Jour., 1860, pp. 223, 298.)

f. When an expelled preacher does not submit to the decision of the conference, but continues to preach as if still in full possession of ministerial powers, and has connected himself with another Church or organization contemplating church ends independent of and hostile to the Methodist Episcopal Church, he is not entitled to an appeal. (Gen. Conf. Jour., 1860, p. 253.)

But in all cases where the right of appeal has not been lost by some violation of the provisions of the Discipline, the appeal must be entertained.

10. If an appeal is well taken, it does not place the case wholly within the jurisdiction of the appellate court to make such an award as it deems proper; but the appellate court must either affirm or reverse the decision of the court below, or remand the case for a new trial. (Bishops Janes and Baker.)

11. Decisions in an appellate court:
"In any ecclesiastical court of appeals, when the three questions, Shall the decision of the

lower court be affirmed? Shall the case be remanded for a new trial? Shall the former decission be reversed? have been successively put, and there is a tie vote on each, then in what condition does it leave the appellant?

"*Resolved*, That it is the sense of this conference that when the motions to affirm, to remand, and to reverse have been successively put and lost, the decision of the court below stands as the final adjudication of the case."—*Gen. Conf. Jour.*, 1860, p. 248.

12. In no case of appeal can new evidence be admitted. Only the journalized and documentary testimony taken and presented at the first trial can be introduced. (Gen. Conf. Jour., 1848, p. 127.) If the appellant affirms that he has in his possession testimony which was not before the original court, and which, in his opinion, would exculpate him from one or more charges on which he was expelled, the case may be remanded for a new trial. (Gen. Conf. Jour., 1840, p. 77.)*

13. Relation of an expelled member whose case has been remanded by the appellate court:

"When an appeal is taken by an expelled member to the quarterly conference, and the

* For further Disciplinary action on Appeals see pp.242-245.

conference remands the case for a new trial, what is the precise relation of the appellant? Is he an accused member, and must the preacher proceed to try him again, or is he restored to his membership in good standing?

Ans. He is an accused member, and the preacher " shall proceed to try him again unless the charges are withdrawn."—*See Discipline,* ¶ 243.

14. After a member has been tried, expelled, and taken an appeal, and the quarterly conference has affirmed the decision of the court below, a succeeding quarterly conference is not competent to reopen the case for adjudication, by granting another trial to the expelled member. The decision of the appellate court is final. (Bishop Hedding.)

15. When the appellate court reverses the decision of the court below, the appellant is reinstated in his former membership, without any action of the court from which he took an appeal.

16. If an excluded steward, exhorter, or class-leader is restored to membership by the quarterly conference, such action does not

restore him to his previous *official* relation. He is brought to trial as if he had sustained no official relation; and a quarterly conference can restore no office which it is not originally empowered to give.

17. When a decision on a point of law is made by a presiding elder in a district or quarterly conference, and action follows which affects the membership of a member of that conference, such action is final, provided that no appeal is taken to the president of the next annual conference. (Bishop Hamline.)

18. No accused lay member can take an appeal until he is excluded from the Church. But when he is once expelled, the act of expulsion stands until the decision is reversed, on appeal, by the quarterly conference. The person thus expelled, though he takes an appeal, cannot enjoy any privileges of society until the decision of the appellate court. And if the quarterly report be read before the appeal is tried, and the decision reversed, the preacher in charge is bound to read him out among those excluded from the Church according to Discipline. If the decision is reversed by the quarterly conference, the preacher in charge

should announce before the society that the person is restored to membership by the act of the quarterly conference. (Bishop Morris.)

19. When an appeal is taken from the decision of an ecclesiastical court, that fact should be entered upon the records of the trial; and the presiding officer is required to present such records, and all the documents relating to the case, to the appellate court. When a traveling preacher, however, has been tried, and has taken an appeal, it is the duty of the secretary of the annual conference to preserve the minutes of the trial, and all the documents relating to it, and transmit them, at the proper time, to the judicial conference.

20. When an appellant does not appear personally, or by a representative, to prosecute his appeal, it goes by default. (Bishop Ames.)

21. If in the examination of an appeal the presiding elder discover that the trial below was informally conducted, he has no authority to throw out the case, prevent the decision of the conference, and declare the person not expelled. The appeal is not to the presiding elder, but to the quarterly conference.

22. If, in the judgment of the presiding elder, because of local prejudice an impartial trial cannot be had in the quarterly conference of the circuit or station where the appellant resides, he may, on the demand of either party, cause the appeal to be tried by any other quarterly conference within his district, after due notice to the complainant and appellant.

SECTION XI.—*New Trial.*

1. It is not in accordance with our usages for a presiding officer to order, under any circumstances, a new trial; but an appellate court may remand an appeal case for a new trial.

2. If the preacher in charge differs in judgment from the majority of the society, or the select number, concerning the guilt or innocence of an accused member, the trial may be referred, by the preacher in charge, to the *ensuing* quarterly conference. But this *reference of the trial* does not place the case before the quarterly conference for adjudication; it is simply a petition for a new trial, and the quarterly conference may grant or reject it according to their best judgment. (Disc.,¶¶ 242, 243.)

3. When the case is remanded for a new trial, it should proceed as if no trial had pre-

viously been held. There must be a new presentation of charges and specifications, a new notifying of the party, hearing of witnesses, and rendering of verdict. Any of the original charges and specifications may be withdrawn, and new charges and specifications may be added. New evidence may be produced, and such documentary testimony as has been taken according to Discipline, and admitted in the first trial, may be introduced in the new trial (Gen. Conf. Jour., 1848, p. 129.)

It would be a flagrant proceeding for the adjudicating body, when a case is remanded for a new trial, to re-expel a member on a verdict of guilt rendered at a previous trial, without a new hearing of testimony. (Bishop Hedding.)

4. In the following cases it would be highly proper for the appellate court to grant a new trial.

a. When the minutes of the trial are so imperfect that the true merits of the case cannot be learned from them.

b. In case of maladministration, or incorrect ruling of the presiding officer.

c. When there have been any improprieties in the select committee, such as determining their verdict by casting lots, or by basing it upon documents which were sent to them, but were not read in the trial.

d. When new and material evidence has been discovered. A new trial should not be granted for mere cumulative evidence.

SECTION XII.—*Trial of Local Preachers.*

1. A local preacher, deacon, or elder, is amenable to the district conference, where one is held, otherwise to the quarterly conference, for the faithful performance of the functions of his office; and in case of manifest neglect of duty should be treated the same as in cases of improper tempers, words, and actions. The person thus offending should be reprehended by his senior in office; and should he fail to reform, one, two, or three faithful friends should be taken as witnesses. If he still persists in his neglect of duty, the conference may proceed to try him, and deprive him of his ministerial office.

2. When a local elder, deacon, or preacher is reported to be guilty of some crime expressly forbidden in the word of God, it is made the duty of the preacher in charge to call him before a committee of local preachers, by whom he shall be acquitted, or, if found guilty, sus-

pended until the next district or quarterly conference, as the case may be. The rule "requires the preacher in charge," says Bishop Morris, "to proceed on *mere report*, whether there be any formal charges or not; to call a committee, which is of the nature of a court of inquiry, to ascertain whether or not there be cause of trial; and if so, it must go to the district or the quarterly conference, as the case may be, the only tribunal that has authority to try the case. And in all practicable cases the preacher in charge should inquire into complaints against local preachers, by a committee, before they come into the conference, or be held responsible for this neglect of duty. But if he neglect it, or fail to obtain a committee, or fail for want of time, that neglect or failure does not deprive the conference of its legal authority to try a local preacher on charges of immorality."

3. Bishop Hedding remarks: "Great care should be taken to appoint a wise, prudent, and impartial committee, consisting, if practicable, of more than three. All suitable means should be employed to have a thorough and fair investigation. And as the final trial of a local preacher is by a body of men most of whom are usually laymen, it is desirable that this com-

mittee should be composed of as many as seven or nine."

4. The committee of local preachers may be called from any circuit or district in the conference. The rule of 1796 required that the local preachers in the neighborhood should be called to constitute this committee. In 1820 they were required to belong to the circuit or district. In 1836 all restrictions in this respect were taken away.

5. The mode of conducting an investigation by a committee, in the case of an accused local preacher, is similar to that of the trial of a member before described. The preacher in charge must preside, and cause exact minutes of the charges, specifications, testimony, and examination to be taken; and if the accused is found guilty, these, together with the decision of the committee, must be laid by him before the district conference where one is held, otherwise before the quarterly conference.

6. The acquittal or suspension of a local preacher, in the primary examination, is by the committee, and not by the preacher in charge.

7. The examination before a committee is not a trial proper on the merits of the case; and hence, if a local preacher is acquitted by the committee, charges and specifications, founded upon the same reports, may be preferred against him at the district conference where one is held, otherwise at the quarterly conference, and he be expelled, if they judge him guilty of crime.

8. The mode of conducting the trial of a local preacher is the same as that above described. The president must appoint a secretary to take regular minutes of the evidence of the trial; "which minutes, when read and approved, shall be signed by the president, and also by the members of the conference who are present, or by a majority of them."

9. The district conference, where one is held, or, if no such conference be held, then the quarterly conference, holds original jurisdiction over local preachers, and hence its decision will not be governed by the primary investigation. Testimony may, in first examinations, have been rejected which the president of the quarterly conference judges to be admissible, and testimony may have been admitted which should be

rejected. Any additional testimony which either party may have obtained may be presented.

10. If the accused refuse or neglect to appear, either before the investigating committee or the conference, he may be tried in his absence.

11. The conference having jurisdiction alone awards punishment in the trial of local preachers. Suspension by the investigating committee is not a penalty judicially awarded, but a public arrest of character until the case can be examined before the proper tribunal. The president cannot expel a local preacher; he merely announces the decision of the conference.

12. If a local preacher has been expelled, and has taken an appeal to the annual conference, a subsequent district or quarterly conference cannot reconsider its action, and restore the local preacher. If a subsequent conference should reconsider the act of a former session, and restore one whom they had expelled, for the same reason they might reconsider and condemn a man whom they had previously acquitted. And if they could reconsider the act of the last conference, they might reconsider an act passed years before. (Bishop Hedding.)

13. When a local preacher has been brought to trial before a district or a quarterly conference, and the evidence has been taken, and the pleadings closed, it is not lawful for the conference to adjourn, and leave the decision of the case to the next conference.

14. A district or a quarterly conference has no authority to alter the language of any charge or specification without the consent of the parties.

15. When the property of a local preacher has accumulated so rapidly as to cause some to suspect that he is not acquiring it honestly, the district or the quarterly conference, of which he is a member, has no authority to demand of him a statement of the amount of his property, and of the manner in which it has been acquired. If he is suspected of dishonesty, he may be arraigned; but the accuser must produce testimony to sustain the charge. No man can be compelled to witness against himself. (Ref. Bishop Soule.)

16. When the matters involved in a bill of charges, presented against a member, local or traveling preacher, in whole or any material

part, are pending before a civil or criminal court, it is frequently advisable to lay the case over until the trial is decided by the legal tribunal. Equity seems to demand it. If in this case the local preacher has been suspended by a committee, and the case is brought before the ensuing district or quarterly conference for trial,—if the conference believe that the charges cannot be fully investigated until after the suits pending before the civil tribunals are terminated,—it is competent to adjourn the case until after such trial. The results, however, of a criminal prosecution ought not to exert any influence on the results of the ecclesiastical investigation. Equity and the honor of the Church might demand the conviction and expulsion of the person whom the civil law had cleared.

17. The fact that a member of a quarterly conference has been employed as counsel in a civil suit against a local preacher does not disqualify him from acting and voting as a member of the district or the quarterly conference, in the trial of the local preacher on charges involving the material facts pending in the civil court. Every member of a district or of a quarterly conference, except while he himself is being tried, may exercise every *right*, and perform

every *act* appertaining to his office, as a member of the conference, if it has no respect to his own personal interests.

18. When charges are preferred against a preacher on trial, the presiding elder has a right to decide under which provision of ¶¶ 223-229 of the Discipline the case shall be tried.

SECTION XIII.—*Trial of Traveling Preachers.*

1. The nature of the investigation of an accused traveling preacher, by a committee, in the interval of an annual conference, is the same as that of a local preacher, above described. It is strictly preliminary in its character. The committee can merely suspend from ministerial services and Church privileges until the ensuing annual conference.

2. " The great object of committees is to attend to complaints, or charges, in the intervals of conferences, and thereby secure the character of innocent brethren, wrongfully accused, from reproach and injury; or [of saving the Church from harm] by suspending [such as are adjudged guilty] until the ensuing conference. And it may be further remarked that neither the or-

ganization of a committee, nor any of their acts, can abridge the powers of a conference, when they afterward come to sit on the same case. And should a case occur at or during the sitting of a conference, or, although known of, be neglected ; or, if it should be of such recent date as not to afford time to call a committee, and should then be brought before the conference, there is nothing in the Discipline, or reason, to prevent the conference from hearing and deciding thereon, without the intervention of a committee; and especially if the person accused desire it. But as the conference has the entire control of all cases in which its own members are concerned, subject to the order of Discipline, they may, or they may not, appoint a committee, as they may judge proper."—*M'Kendree.*

The Restrictive Rules provide that ministers or preachers shall have the privilege " of trial by a committee." This implies that preachers shall not be suspended in the interval of conference, as they formerly were, without the investigation and action of a committee ; but it was not intended to abridge the powers of an annual conference,—it has original jurisdiction over its members.

3. If the charge be preferred at the confer-

ence, the case may be referred to a committee, in the presence of a presiding elder, or a member, appointed by the bishop in his stead. In the latter case, the person so appointed possesses all the powers of a presiding elder in an investigating committee.

4. An annual conference has a right, when charges are preferred against one of its number, and the case cannot be tried during its session, for want of testimony, to refer it to the presiding elder who may have charge of him, under the rule for the trial of immoral ministers, in the interval of an annual conference. When cases are thus referred, the committee possesses no more authority than when it is called, in the interval of conference, by the presiding elder. It can only suspend; and the ensuing annual conference must determine the case. If a specific charge only is referred, the committee must restrict its examination to that particular point; but if the *case* of a preacher is referred, the committee may examine any charge which may be preferred against him.

5. The acquittal of an accused traveling preacher by the investigating committee, as in the case of a local preacher, does not prevent

the same charges being preferred, and a trial held before the annual conference, to which he is originally amenable.

6. If the preacher is found guilty by the committee, he must be suspended by it, and not by the presiding elder. The penitence of the convicted cannot prevent suspension.

7. If a committee is appointed to investigate the case of an accused preacher, and report to the next conference, if the conference is divided, and the committee falls into different conferences, its powers remain the same until its report is heard and accepted.

8. When a presiding elder is called to preside at the investigation of an accused presiding elder, he possesses the same powers as when investigating the case of an accused traveling preacher on his district. He may appoint the committee, and the time and place of holding the investigation. The committee should be called from the district of the accused presiding elder, unless special reasons exist why it should not be done.

9. A presiding elder may appoint the place for the investigation of the case of an accused

traveling preacher beyond the limits of his district, when, in his judgment, the circumstances demand it.

10. A presiding elder cannot call a traveling preacher before an investigating committee, except (1) when he "is under report of being guilty of *some crime* expressly forbidden in the word of God as an unchristian practice, sufficient to exclude a person from the kingdom of grace and glory;" or (2) when he is not "cured" of improper tempers, words, or actions on the first and second admonition; or (3) when he "holds and disseminates doctrines which are contrary to our Articles of Religion," and will not "solemnly engage not to disseminate such erroneous doctrines, in public or in private;" or (4) when he ceases to travel without the consent of the annual conference. Complaints of maladministration must go primarily before the annual conference. (Discipline, ¶ 220.) The presiding elder can only remove such from the charge as do not administer Discipline correctly.

11. The form of trial, in the case of a local or traveling preacher, is the same as that of a member, except in the mode of rendering the verdict. The quarterly and annual conferences

vote first upon the question whether the several specifications, in order, under each charge, are sustained, and then upon the charge, without bringing in a written verdict.

12. If an accused traveling preacher does not appear, either before the committee or the annual conference, the same formality should be observed in his trial as if he were present. Competent counsel should be appointed to conduct his case, and accurate minutes should be kept.

13. When a preacher has been tried in an annual conference, and suspended for one year, the conference cannot at the expiration of that time expel him for the same offense, or continue the suspension for another period. When a member has suffered the punishment which was adjudged by the conference, at the time of his trial, he is deemed clear by the law. (Bishop Hedding.)

14. A preacher under suspension by a committee, called by a presiding elder, has no right to vote on any question, at the ensuing annual conference, previously to the examination of his case. His suspension, being in accordance with

the provisions of the Discipline, continues until it is removed by the conference.

15. When a traveling preacher is so unacceptable, inefficient, or secular, as to be no longer useful in his work, the conference may request him to ask a location, and if he shall refuse to comply with the request, the conference shall bear with him till the session next ensuing, at which time, if he persist in his refusal, the conference may, without formal trial, locate him, without his consent, by a vote of two thirds of the members present and voting. (Dis. of 1880, ¶ 188.) It is a rule of discipline that every traveling preacher shall undergo an annual examination of character; and it is expected that every member will be present at the session of the conference. In case of the location of a preacher without consent, as well as of expulsion, the aggrieved party is not allowed an appeal. But it cannot be too strongly urged, that in all cases where the character of a brother is to be arrested, or his relation changed in the ministry, due notice should be previously given, and efforts made to remove the embarrassments.

16. The secretary of an annual conference must carefully take all the testimony given in the annual conference; documentary testimony

need not be spread upon the journals of the conference, but must be properly filed and preserved. In case of trial, a copy of the charges, specifications, and the final action of the conference, should be entered on the principal conference journal, and such references made to all the testimony and documents used in the trial, that they may be readily found and clearly identified.

17. A committee appointed by an annual conference to try a traveling minister is not authorized to hold its sessions after the final adjournment of the conference. The committee of trial is the representative of the annual conference, and subject to its laws of action; and hence cannot perpetuate its existence after the official adjournment of the body which created it.—*Gen. Conf. Jour.*, 1864, p. 232.

SECTION XIV.—*Church Offenses.*

1. In every Church trial it should be definitely stated under what rule of discipline the case is to be tried.

2. All actionable offenses may be brought under one of the following rules:

a. A *crime* expressly forbidden by the word of God, sufficient to exclude a person from the kingdom of grace and glory.

b. Neglect of duties and of the means of grace; imprudent conduct; indulging sinful words, tempers, or actions; the buying, selling, or using of intoxicating liquors as a beverage; dancing, playing at games of chance, attending theaters, horse-races, circuses, dancing-parties, or patronizing dancing-schools, or taking such other amusements as are obviously of misleading or questionable moral tendency, or disobedience to the order and discipline of the Church.

c. Endeavoring to sow dissensions in our societies by inveighing against either our doctrines or discipline.

d. Behaving dishonestly in business transactions, or contracting debts without a probability of paying them.

e. Refusing to refer to arbitration disputed pecuniary questions, when recommended by the preacher in charge; refusing to abide by the judgment of arbiters; entering into law-suits with another member, against the provisions of the Discipline.

3. If the offense belong to the first class, no Church labor is necessary before the presenta-

tion of the charge; in all other cases specific preliminary steps must be taken.

4. If a preacher holds and disseminates doctrines contrary to our Articles of Religion, and persists therein, he may be suspended by a committee, and tried at the annual conference. If his error, however, is a mere matter of opinion, not embraced in our Articles of Religion, he may be borne with in the interval of conference, and his case brought before the annual conference.

The twenty-five Articles of Religion do not embrace all that is included in "our present existing and established standards of doctrine." Many of the characteristic doctrines of our Church are not even referred to directly in those articles. Many of our leading articles of religion are expressed in a negative form, and have special reference to the errors of the Papal Church. Bishop Burnet remarks, that since "the Church of Rome owns all that is positive in our doctrine, there could be no discrimination made but by condemning the most important additions which they have brought into the Christian religion in express words." The Discipline does not expressly state what are our "established standards of doctrine;" but usage and general consent would probably designate Mr. Wesley's Sermons, and his Notes on the New Testament, and Watson's Theological Institutes.

5. The rule respecting members of our Church inveighing against our doctrines and discipline is not to be understood in the sense that they must be brought before a committee, and found guilty of this offense, before they can even be reproved by the senior minister of the circuit. The reproof is to be given, not as a judicial act by the adjudicating body, but simply as the act of the pastor, in the faithful discharge of the duties of the pastorate, and to be performed by him when he is clearly convinced that the accused has really endeavored to sow dissensions in the Church. If the member " persists in such pernicious practices " after reproof is thus administered, he should be brought to trial on a complaint setting forth the nature of his offense.

6. When a charge of slander is preferred by one member against another, it is lawful for the accused to prove the truth of his statements as a ground of justification.

7. But when a member is accused of uttering sinful words in reference to a member, it is not lawful to attempt to prove their truthfulness.

8. No charges for slander can be received except from the person alleged to be slandered, or from his representative; but charges involving defamation of character received from other persons must be for evil speaking, and the truth of such declarations cannot be given in evidence, as it would involve an absent person.

Section XV.—*Penalty.*

1. Church penalty is designed to operate as a motive upon the members to observe correct moral conduct, and to declare the purity of the Church by her efforts to maintain correct principles. To secure these objects it is not so necessary that the punishment should be severe as that it should be certain. It is impossible to graduate the punishment according to the true demerit of the offense, and hence as mild measures should be pursued as possible, and yet show that the Church does not connive at sin, and seek to conceal corruption rather than to purge it away.

2. The following awards should be given, according to different circumstances:

a. A declaration of the guilt of the accused, while forgiveness is extended to the penitent.

b. Censure, or reproof.

c. Suspension.

d. Expulsion.

3. *Forgiveness.* The Church is competent to forgive an offender, when the ends of moral discipline can be promoted by it. Bishop Hedding remarks: "It is asked, Must he expel in all cases? Is there no room for pardon? For scandalous crimes expulsion should undoubtedly take place; but for crimes of a moderate degree, and when the offender is suitably humble and penitent, forgiveness and forbearance should be exercised, and a repentant brother may be retained in the Church. 'Brethren, if any man be overtaken in a fault, ye which are spiritual restore such a one in the spirit of meekness.' Gal. vi, 1. That the rule is to be so understood is evident from a clause in the General Rules, (¶ 35:) 'If there be any among us who observes them not, who habitually breaks any of them, let it be known unto them who watch over that soul as they who must give an account. We will bear with him for a season,

but if then he repent not, he hath no more place among us ; we have delivered our souls.' "—*Discourse on Discipline*, pp. 66, 67. "In exercising mercy, in this case, the preacher will need great prudence to avoid doing it in a way to grieve and afflict the members, or cast a stumbling-block before the world. On this question he should take counsel with the select number, or the leaders' meeting, or in some cases with the society in the place, that it may be understood that the offender is restored by general consent."—*Discourse on Discipline*, pp. 68, 69.

Bishop M'Kendree remarks : " When a person is clearly convicted of such a crime or crimes, (such as are expressly forbidden in the word of God,) nothing short of expulsion will satisfy the rule, unless there be such a manifestation of genuine repentance and humiliation as will fully justify the restoration of the offending person : in such a case the connection between crime and its punishment is dissolved. Such cases may possibly occur, and when they do, much care and prudence are necessary to guard the Church from reproach and injury, and at the same time to save the offender."

4. That the Discipline contemplates that censure and suspension may be inflicted as a Church

penalty upon disorderly members, as well as upon convicted local and traveling preachers, is evident from various considerations. The heading of the section respecting disorderly members was, in its first introduction into the Discipline in 1789, " Of bringing to trial, finding guilty, *reproving, suspending*, or excluding disorderly persons," etc. The section relating to the "sale and use of spirituous liquors," which formed a part of the Discipline from 1796 to 1840, provided that an accused person should " be cleared, *censured, suspended*, or excluded, according to his conduct, as on *other* charges of immorality."

5. No member can be suspended for a particular offense without a regular trial according to Discipline; and no preacher can be suspended by an annual conference beyond the period of one year.

6. When a bill of charges is correctly drawn, the penalty must be based upon the charges which are sustained against the accused. No member can be punished for any higher offense than is charged against him in the bill; but punishment may be awarded for any lower of

fense, of which he is convicted, in the specifications which are sustained against him.

7. "It has been asked," remarks Bishop Hedding, "Has a preacher a right to keep members of the Church, who have not been tried or censured, out of love-feast, or to repel them from the Lord's Supper, for any little irregularity in dress, or otherwise, which he may perceive in them at any time? No; in ordinary cases he has no such right: he may not punish members except as the law directs. Yet there may be *extraordinary* cases which might admit of this measure, from his authority as a minister, without any direct rule. For example: a member is known to have committed a scandalous crime, and there has not been time to call him to trial in the regular way. He comes to love-feast, or to the holy sacrament; in these circumstances the minister may repel him."—*Discourse on Discipline*, p. 72.

8. When a preacher is judged guilty of maladministration by an annual conference, censure and reproof are the highest penalty which they can inflict.

9. When a member or preacher has been expelled, according to due form of Discipline,

he cannot afterward enjoy the privileges of society and of sacraments, in our Church, without contrition, confession, and satisfactory reformation; but if, however, the society become convinced of the *innocence* of an expelled lay member, he may again be received on trial without confession. No expelled member can be received again into full membership without a subsequent probation.

10. When an annual conference decides that a preacher having charge has expelled a member contrary to the provisions of the Discipline, such decision restores the person so expelled to Church-membership. The conference must decide within what time the alleged maladministration must have taken place, to bring it properly before them. (Gen. Conf. Jour., 1852, p. 73.)

11. If the society or select number renders a verdict of guilty, it is not optional with the preacher whether he will expel the offender; as an administrator of the Discipline, he must pronounce the penalty of the law. The Discipline says, " Let the preacher in charge expel him." An exception, however, should be made in those cases where, in view of peculiar palliating circumstances, or the deep penitence of the accused,

the committee or society recommends that he be still further borne with.

12. The practice of requiring a *public* personal confession before the Church, or threatening expulsion if it is not made, is of doubtful expediency. If the accused is really penitent, this can be ascertained in some other mode. The Church, when not under the peculiar sympathy which the presence of the offender might produce, is better prepared to decide whether the concessions and acknowledgments of the accused are sufficient to secure the honor of the Church if expulsion is not inflicted. Many persons, especially under the mortification of the alleged offense, are wholly incapable of making an appropriate statement to the Church in person.

13. 'It is made the duty of the preacher in charge, at every quarterly meeting, to read the names of those who have been excluded from the Church during the preceding quarter; but the Discipline does not contemplate that their crimes—the grounds of Church action—shall be publicly announced, nor that any unusual publicity should be given to the fact of expulsion. When persons are thus read out of the society in the hearing of those who have an interest in

the communication, and a right to know the action of the Church, it is not legal defamation of character, nor *prima facie* evidence of malice.

14. When a member is found guilty of imprudent conduct, and required to make confession, and refuses to comply, the preacher cannot expel him without a further trial before a committee, showing that he does not comply.

Section XVI.—*Arbitration.*

1. In 1781 it was made the duty of the assistant, at the quarterly meeting, to consult with the steward in appointing proper persons to examine into the circumstances where there was a dispute respecting pecuniary matters; and if there was suspicion of injustice, or inability, in the referees, to appoint men of more skill and probity: and the parties were then required to abide by their decision, or be excluded from the society.

In 1784 the Discipline required the assistant to consult with the stewards and leaders, and appoint referees, whose decision was final; and the party refusing to abide by it was to be expelled, unless there appeared to the assistant some fraud or gross mistake in the decision; in which case he was to appoint new referees for a rehearing of the case, and the decision of this tribunal was to be absolutely final.

2. Under our present rule, the authority of the preacher is greatly diminished; yet he has discretionary power to decide—

a. Whether the circumstances require any action. The rule does not oblige him to recommend arbitration, unless he judges that the case is such as strictly to demand such investigation.

b. If proceedings should be commenced, under what rule of Discipline the action should be brought,—whether it is an immorality, an indiscretion, or a dispute respecting the paymen⁴ of debts, etc. (Bishop Morris.)

3. The phrase "business transactions" is to be restricted entirely to pecuniary matters. But it embraces them in all their forms, whether relating to real or personal estate, debts, demands, accounts, or contracts.

4. The arbiters to whom the case is referred must be members of the Methodist Episcopal Church; but the arbitration does not assume the form of a trial, and it is not necessary that

the arbiters should belong to the society with which either of the parties is connected.

5. The preacher in charge should preside at the arbitration, when both of the parties belong to the same society. If they belong to different societies, Christian and ministerial etiquette would seem to require that the senior preacher should preside.

6. Order of conducting an arbitration.
a. Religious services.
b. Appointment of secretary by the referees.
c. The complainant makes his statement, introducing such testimony as he deems proper.
d. The defendant makes his answer, and introduces his testimony.
e. Rebutting testimony by the complainant.
f. Rebutting testimony by the defendant.
g. Closing arguments,—
   (1.) By the complainant.
   (2.) By the defendant.
h. The parties should then retire, and the decision should be written and signed by the referees.

7. The rule does not require our members to arbitrate when the other party is not a member of our Church.

8. When a dispute respecting pecuniary matters arises between a member of our Church and a firm or corporation, to which one or more members of our Church belongs, the rule respecting arbitration does not apply; for the corporation, as such, is not under the control of the Church. For any unjustifiable business transaction, performed by the member, or by the firm, which the member could have controlled, he should be held strictly accountable.

9. A member refusing to arbitrate when recommended to do so by the preacher in charge, renders himself liable to expulsion from the Church; but in this, as in all other cases, he cannot be expelled until a select number, in due form, declare that he refuses to arbitrate, or has violated some express rule of Church covenant.

10. If a preacher or member shall enter into a lawsuit with another member before the matter is submitted to arbitration, he does so on his own responsibility; and, if arrested, must show that the case was of such a nature as to require and justify a process at law.

11. The inspecting of the accounts of those who "fail in business," and the calling of a

debtor before a committee, to show cause why he does not make payment, are not Church trials; and a member cannot be expelled merely on those examinations, whatever fraud and dishonesty those examinations may disclose. But if these examinations should disclose frauds, a bill of charges should be formed from them, and the accused brought to trial, in due form, before a select committee.

CHAPTER VI.
CHURCH PROPERTY.

SECTION I.—*Building Churches and Parsonages.*

1. THE Discipline expressly discountenances the incurring of heavy liabilities in the erection of churches and parsonages. Hence it is made the duty of the quarterly conference, where it is contemplated to build a house of worship, to secure the lot on which such house is to be erected, according to our deed of settlement· and also "to appoint a judicious committee of at least, three members of our Church, to form an estimate of the amount necessary to build; and three fourths of the money, according to such estimate, must be secured, or subscribed, before any such building shall be commenced." " In all cases where debts for building houses of worship have been, or may be, incurred contrary to, or in disregard of, the above recommendation, our members and friends are requested to discountenance, by declining pecuniary aid to, all agents who travel beyond their own circuits or districts for the collection of funds for the dis-

charge of such debts, except in such peculiar cases as may be approved by an annual conference, or such agents as may be appointed by their authority."

2. When a number of persons have associated themselves together, in pursuance of the statute, for the purpose of erecting a meeting-house, and appointed three or more of their number a building committee, to superintend the erection of the house, the mere acceptance of the appointment does not amount to a personal undertaking, on the part of the committee, to build the house; but the only effect is to constitute them the agents and representatives of the association, to act upon joint consideration and advice, with power to make all necessary contracts, and authorize all such expenditures as the purposes of the agency require.

If the building committee are the agents of an unincorporated body, and in making their contracts do not pledge their individual credit and responsibility, they will not be held under a personal obligation for such indebtedness, if at the time of the contract the nature of their agency was definitely known.

And if the committee should contract with one of their own number, they would as effect-nally bind the society as if they contracted with a stranger. (Ref. 3 Vt. Rep., 431; 2 Washburn, 593; 3 ibid., 405.)

3. Where the articles of association provided that the whole expense of the house should be estimated on the whole number of pews, by appraisal, and that the subscribers should bid for their choice of pews, but that the average price of the pews should not exceed a certain sum, this could not be construed as limiting the amount to be expended by the building committee in erecting the house; and a member of the committee might recover for services and expenditures in erecting the building, notwithstanding the whole expense of the house exceeded the amount which the pews would bring at the average price specified, if it could be shown that the building committee had not departed from the general plan prescribed for the building. (Ibid.)

SECTION II.—*Trustees.*

1. All our Church property, such as meetinghouses, parsonages, and cemeteries, held according to Discipline, is vested in a board of trustees, who hold it in trust for the use of the members

of the Methodist Episcopal Church. The ministry, either in their individual or associated capacity, as Annual or General Conferences, have never claimed, nor do they hold, in law, any title to any chapel or parsonage by the deed of settlement. The fee of the land is vested in trustees, who hold the property in behalf of each respective society. The General Conference claims merely the right to supply the pulpit, by such means as it shall elect, with duly accredited ministers and preachers of the Methodist Episcopal Church, " who shall preach and expound God's holy word therein." The General Conference of 1796, referring to the deed of settlement, adopted the following sentiments: " By which we manifest to the whole world that the property of the preaching-houses will not be invested in the General Conference. But the preservation of our union, and the progress of the work of God, indispensably require that the free and full use of the pulpit should be in the hands of the General Conference and the yearly conferences authorized by them. Of course, the traveling preachers who are in full connection, assembled in their conferences, are the patrons of the pulpits of our churches."— *Gen. Conf. Jour.*, vol. i, p. 15. Whenever it becomes necessary, for the payment of debts, or with a view to reinvestment, to make a sale of church property, the proceeds of the sale, after the payment of debts, must be applied to the purchase or improvement of other property for the same uses, and deeded to the Church in the same manner, according to the judgment of the quarterly conference *for the use of the said society.*

2. Where the law of the State or Territory prescribes no specified mode of election, trustees must be elected annually by the fourth quarterly conference of the circuit or station, upon the nomination of the preacher in charge, or the presiding elder of the district.

In all meetings of trustees, thus appointed, the stationed preacher, by general usage, is *ex officio* the presiding officer.

3. To be eligible as a trustee, a person must be, at least, twenty-one years of age, and a majority of every board of trustees must be members of the Methodist Episcopal Church. No trustee can be ejected from office while he is in joint security for money, unless such relief be given him as is demanded, or the creditor will accept:

4. The great and paramount duty of trustees of religious corporations is to see that the temporalities committed to their charge are fully and fairly devoted to the purposes which the founders had in view in creating the trust. All their authority is necessarily subordinate to this end, and all exercise of it beyond the legitimate attainment of this end is usurpation.

As the deed of settlement secures the use of the pulpit, "to preach and expound God's holy word therein," to such ministers and preachers of the Methodist Episcopal Church as the General Conference shall duly authorize, if the trustees should refuse to receive them, and shut the doors of the church against them, the court would issue a peremptory mandamus commanding them to admit the preacher thus appointed into the church.

It is no valid excuse for the trustees to say that a majority of the members of the Church direct them to close the doors, and sustain them in the act. "They are not chosen to represent that majority, but rather to execute the trust of carrying out the intention of those from whose benevolence flow the temporalities put in their charge. If such an excuse will ever be available, where will it stop? What shall set bounds to its encroachment? They from whose benevolence has arisen some pious foundation, or some noble charity, may have passed from the stage of life, leaving behind them some such monument of their love to God and man, in the confident expectation that the trust they have confided to posterity will be faithfully executed. Upon what principle can it be justified, that they who now live to enjoy the fruits of the charity of the dead should be permitted, at their caprice, to control, and perhaps divert from its original purpose, the endowment which owes none of its support to them? No such principle is known in law or morals."—2 *Barbour*, pp. 414, 415.

5. The trustees of an incorporated religious society are, *virtute officii*, entitled to the possession of all the temporalities of the society, and are considered as lawfully seized of the grounds and buildings of the Church; and hence, if the trustees should close the doors of the church against the minister and congregation, they have no right to make a forcible entry into the church. The merit or demerit of the trustees in closing the doors of the church cannot be taken into consideration in this case. If the trustees have violated their trust, the society has ample remedy; but this remedy does not consist in a forci-

ble entry upon their possessions. While the trustees are in actual possession, the civil authority is bound to protect them against the unlawful and irregular intrusion of any persons, whether members of the Church or strangers. The trustees are responsible for the faithful discharge of their trust, not to a violent mob, but to the society, in a legal manner, whose interests they serve. (Ref. 9 Johnson, 156.)

6. A church is erected for the public worship of God, and the moral and religious instruction of the people; and the trustees have no authority to make use of the church, at such intervals as it is not occupied by the pastor, for purposes at variance with the object for which it was erected.

7. Trustees can legally protect the church property against all lawless violence and injury, even if the society has never been legally incorporated, and may maintain an action against the trespasser for the injury which is done. (Ref. 9 Wendall, 414.)

8. Where the officers of a religious corporation are required by their charter to be annually elected, they would, probably, be allowed to

exercise their office after the expiration of the year, provided an election had not taken place to fill the vacancy. This case is provided for in some of the States by express statutes, and such has been the general ruling of the courts.

9. The power of trustees in the Methodist Episcopal Church seems to be restricted to the holding of real estate, and such personal property as has been raised or acquired for the benefit alone of the temporalities of the Church. They may take up subscriptions and collections for the purpose of creating church property, for the payment of debts previously contracted, and for repairing and improving the real estate of the society; but they have no authority to forbid the stewards raising voluntary contributions for the support of the Gospel and the various benevolent institutions of the Church, nor can they claim that the funds raised for these purposes, either in the classes or in the public congregation, shall be deposited in their hands. Our economy requires that these funds shall be disbursed by the stewards, and the trustees cannot exercise their powers in such a manner as to defeat the very purposes of their creation. (Bangs's His. M. E. Church, vol. iv, pp. 175-181.)

10. The board of trustees is responsible to the quarterly conference of the circuit or station, and is required to present a report, annually, of its acts during the preceding year; hence the quarterly conference must see that all vacancies in the board of trust are duly filled, and that the corporation does not in any instance transcend its powers, or fail to discharge the obligations of its trust. In case it is necessary to take any legal steps to check the action of the trustees, the quarterly conference is the proper body to give instruction upon this subject.

11. Corporations created for a specific object have no power to take and hold real estate for purposes wholly foreign to that object. (3 Pickering, 232–240.)

Section III.—*Pews.*

1. We do not propose in this section to consider the question of the propriety of building churches with pews; but as such churches exist among us it is a practical question, What is the nature of the claim which a pew-holder possesses to a pew in a house of worship?

The society, or its representatives, the trustees, own the fee of the land on which the house is erected. By a grant of a pew, the grantee acquires only a qualified usufructuary right. He can claim no interest in the soil beneath his pew, nor in the space above it, nor an absolute claim to any part of the building itself. The society can control the soil, can construct a gallery and pews above him, and prevent the pew-holder from removing the material of his pew from the house. The right of the pew-owner is limited as to time. If the house be burned, or destroyed by time, the right is lost. The grant of a pew does not bind the society to provide for the maintenance of public worship in the meeting-house; but they may abandon it at pleasure. It is the opinion, also, of able jurists that the rights of a pew-owner are subject to the right of the society to remove the house to such a location as will best accommodate the whole congregation. In this case the value of the property is not diminished, but rather enhanced by the more commodious location of the house. But the pew-owner does acquire the exclusive right to occupy his pew when the house is opened for public religious worship. He may exclude all other persons from his pew, by fastening the pew-door, provided he does not annoy those who occupy other pews in the house; and if a person enters a pew when he knows that the owner forbids any such entry, he becomes a trespasser, and liable to an action for such entry. (See 17 Mass. Rep., 435; 1 Pickering, 102; 24 Pickering, 347; 4 N. H. Rep., 181, 182; 3 Washburn, 266, 277; 5 Metcalf, 127; 5 Cowen, 496; 19 Pickering, 361.)

2. When a meeting-house is conveyed to trustees for the use of a certain Church or society for a place of worship, and for no other use, intent, or purpose, whatsoever, and in the deeds of the pews to individuals the provisions of the conveyance of the house are referred to and recognized, the pew-owner has a right, probably, to the occupancy of his pew whenever the house is publicly opened, though it is opened for purposes different from those mentioned in the conveyance; nor can the trustees expel him from his pew on any public occasion. "It is the practice," however, as Judge Shaw remarks, "for religious societies to lend the use of their houses to various societies and philanthropic associations, to hold meetings for various purposes, and upon such occasions it has been usual for the body or association to whom the house is lent to control the use of the pews, without regard to particular owners. Perhaps loans of the use of houses of worship may be resolved

into a mere practice of courtesy on the part of religious societies, and of voluntary acquiescence on the part of pew-owners, not affecting the legal rights of either."—5 *Metcalf*, 133.

3. No pew-owner has a right to use his pew for any purpose incompatible with the purpose for which the house was erected; and if he should put any offensive covering over his pew, the trustees have a right to remove it; but if, in removing it, they should do any unnecessary injury to the pew, they would become liable to an action for trespass. (5 Metcalf, 127.)

4. When a house of worship is taken down as a matter of necessity, because it has become ruinous, and wholly unfit for the purposes for which it was erected, the trustees are not liable to make any compensation to the pew-owners, but may take the avails of the materials of which the house was constructed for the purpose of erecting another house in its place; but if the house is taken down to render it more convenient and tasteful, or if in rebuilding the pews are destroyed for a useful purpose, an indemnity must probably be made to the pew-owner. (Ref. 3 Washburn, 266; 19 Pickering, 361; 17 Mass. Rep., 435.)

If, however, the trustees, after having taken all legal steps, should remove a pew, and make a tender to the owner of the value of his pew, his action would be barred for damages. (24 Pickering, 347.)

5. The interest of a person in a pew in a house of worship, although limited and qualified, yet is of such a character that a contract for a pew, for a period extending beyond one year, would probably be void unless reduced to writing. (16 Wendall, 28.)

6. Pews are regarded in some States as real estate, in others as personal. In New Hampshire they are deemed personal property, and may be attached by leaving an attested copy of the writ, and of the officer's return thereon, with the town clerk of the town in which such meeting-house is, provided the debtor's interest in one pew, in any meeting-house in which he or his family usually worship, shall be exempt from attachment. (R. S., chap. 184.)

7. Houses of worship, pews, and their furniture, are exempt from taxation in nearly all the States of the Union.

8. Selling pews at auction. The auctioneer, though a trustee, is the agent for both parties— for the purchaser, as explicitly as for the trustees. The bidder announces his bid for the purpose that the auctioneer may write his name against the pew to be sold; and when the entry is made the contract is signed by an agent for the purchaser, which renders it legally binding. But the memorandum of the sale must be perfect: the conditions must be specified, and all the papers must be attached together. The mere writing of the name of the purchaser on the ground-plan of the pews, with the amount which is bid, is not sufficient. (16 Wendall, 28.)

9. Form of deed. In a quit-claim deed, of ordinary form, insert the following description:

" The pew or seat in the Methodist Episcopa. Church in the said L——, which is numbered ——, with all the privileges and appurtenances, estate, right, title, interest, and property of us, or of either of us, whatsoever, as trustees for and in behalf of the said Methodist Episcopal society: reserving to the said Methodist Episcopal society the sole use of the said church as a place of religious worship, according to the rules and discipline which from time to time may be agreed upon at their General Conferences; and also reserving to the said Methodist Episcopal society the sole use of the said pew during the holding of love-feasts, class-meetings, and such special Church meetings as the duly-authorized ministers of the Methodist Episcopal Church shall appoint; and also reserving unto the said Methodist Episcopal society the right to levy a proportionate tax upon said pew for the necessary repairs and insurance of the house." Signed, sealed, witnessed, and acknowledged in due form.

Section IV.—*Subscription Papers.*

1. No particular form is required to render a subscription legal. The object and conditions of the subscription should be clearly and explicitly stated, and it should be made payable to a body competent to contract. A pecuniary consideration need not to be mentioned to render the subscription valid : there should be implied mutual promises. The expending of money, or the undertaking by one party to accomplish an object which both desire. is a legal consideration for the promise of the other. Subscriptions for the purchase or improvement of real estate should be made payable to the board of trustees, when such trustees exist.

2. When a person, by a voluntary subscription, promises to pay in labor or materials, at his option, during another season, for the erection of a public building, and who can be presumed to know that the building is being erected, a demand on him for the labor or materials, previous to the completion of the house, is not necessary. A demand made after the building is finished is sufficient, if the payee is willing to receive such pay at the place where the building is erected, or at any other place equally convenient for the promiser. If the promiser, in such a case, wishes to free himself from his obligation, he must make an offer of payment to the committee appointed to erect said building, or to the person or persons to whom his subscription has been assigned. (Ref. 2 Vt. Reports, 48.)

3. When a conditional subscription is drawn, it should be so expressed that the corporation should virtually be requested by the promiser to perform certain acts, or fulfill certain conditions. Instead of saying that the amount subscribed is not to be paid until $50,000 are subscribed, it should read, Provided the corporation should procure subscriptions to the amount of $50,000, and should afterward invest

the money in a particular mode. (Ref. 1 Comstock, pp. 581-585.)

4. Fictitious subscriptions, obtained for the purpose of inducing others to subscribe more largely, render void those subscriptions which follow them. (1 Vt. Rep., 189-212.)

5. When an authorized agent makes a deduction in collecting a subscription to a person to whom he thinks it is entitled, it does not invalidate the other subscriptions. (Id.)

6. If the purpose for which the subscription was raised was never attempted in any manner to be executed, the promiser would not be obligated to pay his subscription.

CHAPTER VII.

MINISTERIAL SUPPORT

SECTION I.—*Allowance.*

1. The salaries of ministers are fixed by representatives of the people whom they serve.

The following schedule will show the maximum annual amount allowed to the preacher and his family at different periods of the Church:

	1774.	1778.	1780.	1784.	1800.	1816.	1824-60
Preacher....	£24 Penn.	£32 Va.	£32 Va.	£24 Penn.	$80†	$100†	$100†
Preacher's wife......	......	......	£32*	£24*	$80	$100	$100
Child under 7 years	......	......	......	£6	$16	$16	$16
Child from 7 to 14 years.	......	......	......	£8	$24	$24	$24
Orphans of Preachers..	......	......	......	......	$16*	$16*	‡

* Conditionally. † And travelling expenses.
‡ The same as children of living preachers, according to their age.

2. The following plan was adopted by the General Conference of 1872 for the support of our ministry, and the widows and children of deceased ministers:

The Support of Bishops, and the Families of Deceased Bishops.

The General Conference shall determine which of the bishops are effective, and which are non-effective.

It shall be the duty of the Book Committee to make an estimate of the amount necessary to furnish a competent support to each effective bishop, considering the number and condition of his family; and the amount, if any, necessary to the comfortable maintenance of the non-effective bishops; and also the amount necessary to assist the widows and children of deceased bishops; and the bishops are authorized to draw on the treasurer of the Episcopal Fund for said amount, and also for their traveling expenses.

The bishop presiding at an annual conference, within whose bounds a widow or orphan of a deceased bishop may reside, shall be authorized to draw on the treasurer of the Episcopal Fund for such amount as may be estimated as aforesaid.

The Book Committee shall divide the aggregate sum required to be raised for these purposes among the annual conferences, on the basis of the total amount raised in the respective annual conferences for ministerial support, exclusive of missionary appropriations; and the annual conferences shall apportion the same to the several districts; and the district stewards to the several charges. (See Discipline, ¶ 361.) The amount apportioned to each pastoral charge for the support of the bishops shall be a *pro rata* claim with that of the stationed preachers and presiding elders, and no such preacher or presiding elder shall be entitled to his allowance except to the extent to which the claims of the bishops are met by the station or district with which he is connected. And it shall be the duty of the annual conferences to see that the amounts apportioned to the different pastoral charges for the support of the bishops are raised and forwarded quarterly, when practicable, to the Treasurer of the Episcopal Fund.

The Treasurer shall charge the sums paid to the bishops, and to the widows and children of deceased bishops, to "The Episcopal Fund," and all collections received from the different charges for the support of the bishops shall be credited to said fund. And the Treasurer shall report annually to the annual conferences the amounts received from the several annual conferences on account of said fund, and also the expenditures made; and he shall also make a full and detailed exhibit of such receipts and expenditures for the term of four years to the General Conference.

Support of Presiding Elders.

There shall be annually, in every district, a meeting composed of one steward from each circuit and station, to be selected by the quarterly conference, whose duty it shall be, with the advice of the presiding elder, (who shall preside in such meeting,) to make an estimate of the amount necessary to furnish a comfortable support to the presiding elder, and to apportion the same, including house-rent and traveling expenses, and also the claim of the bishops assessed to the district by the annual conference, among the different circuits and stations in the district, according to their several ability ; and in all cases the presiding elder shall share with the bishop and preachers in his district in proportion with what they have respectively received ; but if there be a surplus of money raised, he shall receive such surplus, provided he do not receive more than his allowance.

Support of Ministers and Preachers.

It shall be the duty of the quarterly conference of each circuit and station, at the session immediately preceding the annual conference, to appoint an estimating committee, who shall make an estimate of the amount necessary to furnish a comfortable support to the preacher or preachers stationed among them, taking into consideration the number and condition of the family or families of such preacher or preachers, which estimate shall be subject to the action of the quarterly conference; and to which shall be added the amount apportioned for the support of the bishops and presiding elder; and the stewards shall provide by such methods as they may judge best to meet such amount. The traveling and moving expenses of the preachers shall not be reckoned as a part of the estimate, but be paid by the stewards separately. The quarterly conference shall also make provision for the support of any superannuated preacher, or the widow or child of any deceased preacher, within its bounds, and shall send estimate to the annual conference with which claimant is connected.

Methods of making up any Deficiency.

The more effectually to raise the amount necessary to meet the above-mentioned allowances of the effective ministers and preachers, let the stewards estimate the amount needed monthly. Then ascertain from each member of the Church, and, as far as practicable, from each attendant of the congregation, what each will give toward such expenses.

Let these sums be entered by the recording

steward in a book which he shall keep as treasurer of the board of stewards. If the total amount of these sums does not equal the amount needed monthly, then let the stewards apportion the deficiency among all such as are willing, for Christ's sake, to assume such deficiency, setting down to each person, with his consent, the additional amount which they think he ought monthly to pay.

Let the stewards then adopt and carry out a plan by which every one—except such as prefer to make weekly contributions through their class-leaders—shall have the opportunity of regularly contributing each month, or oftener, not grudgingly nor of necessity, the sum which has been pledged by him. Let these contributions be paid over regularly to the recording steward or class-leader, and be brought up by him to the leaders' meeting or quarterly conference, as the case may be. The recording steward shall keep an individual account of all these pledges and contributions, and shall pay over the same, under the direction of the stewards, to the preachers authorized to receive them.

To provide to meet the claims that may be presented and determined at the annual conference, every preacher shall make an annual collection in every congregation of his charge, and the money so collected shall be lodged in the hands of the steward or stewards, and brought or sent to the ensuing annual conference.

3. The Chartered Fund was established in 1776, and was designed to relieve the distresses and supply the deficiencies of the itinerant and superannuated ministers and preachers of the Methodist Episcopal Church in the United States of America, who remain in connection with, and continue subject to the order and control of, the General Conference, and also for the relief of the wives and children, widows and orphans, of such preachers. The amount of the invested funds, as reported in 1884, is $46,284 20. The income is divided equally among the several annual conferences, now amounting to more than one hundred.

4. There is no specific rule which determines what shall constitute traveling expenses. This matter is very wisely left for the stewards and preacher to arrange, subject to a reference to the quarterly conference.

5. The traveling expenses of editors appointed by the General Conference include those expenses only which are incurred by moving to the place of their appointment, and in going

to and returning from the annual sessions of the conferences of which they are members. (Gen. Conf. Jour., 1848, pp. 112, 113.)

6. The rule authorizing the appointment of an estimating committee was formed by the General Conference of 1816. This committee must be composed of members of the Church; but the rule does not require that they should be members of the quarterly conference.

It is required that this committee be appointed at the last quarterly conference in each ecclesiastical year, that it may be prepared to present its report to the first quarterly conference in the conference year.

The report of the estimating committee is subject to the action of the quarterly conference, and hence it may increase or diminish the estimated amount.

In making its estimate the committee should simply consider the question, What is a suitable amount to furnish a comfortable support for the preacher or preachers stationed among them? Every circumstance should be duly considered: the condition of the preacher's family, whether sickly or otherwise; the state of the market, and the expensiveness of the place where the preacher resides. The social position of the preacher should not be overlooked. He should be enabled to live respectably among his congregation, and not be so reduced, by a stinted policy, that he who should not be unmindful to entertain strangers be necessitated to turn away angels from his door.

7. Whenever any claimant on the funds of a conference shall be in debt to the Book Concern, the conference of which he is a member has power to appropriate the amount of such claim, or any part of it, to the payment of said debt.

8. It is general usage for the society to pay any expenses which may be incurred in supplying the pulpit on the Sabbath in which the preacher is absent at the annual conference.

9. When a preacher is absent from his charge, in obedience to the authority of the Church, as delegate to the General Conference, member of the General Mission Committee, etc., he is entitled to his full salary as a regular pastor.

10. When an effective preacher, by the appointment of the bishop and the recommendation of an annual conference, serves a corporation as professor, agent of the American Bible

Society, etc., it is understood that he has made a specific stipulation in regard to his support and that he thereby releases his claim, while employed in such service, on the conference funds.

11. "When a member of the annual conference is accused of crime in the interval of his conference sessions, and is suspended by a committee and subsequently convicted by his conference, and expelled, his claim upon the funds of the conference shall cease from the time of his suspension."—*Gen. Conf. Jour.*, 1860, p. 303.

A violation of covenant vows works a forfeiture of all disciplinary claims.

12. The claim of a widow of a traveling preacher on the funds of the conference does not depend upon her Christian character, or her connection with the Methodist Episcopal Church; but if she marries she ceases to be a claimant.

13. The British Wesleyan Connection has a specific rule that those preachers who marry widows having issue by their former husbands, shall have no assistance, either from the public

funds or from the circuits in which they labor for the children of the former marriage. Such is the usage among us. But a child legally adopted by a preacher is a disciplinary claimant upon the funds of the conference.

Section II.—*Stewards.*

1. The following is Mr. Wesley's account of the origin of stewards: "In a few days some of them said, 'Sir, we will not sit under you for nothing; we will subscribe quarterly.' I said, 'I will have nothing, for I want nothing. My fellowship supplies me with all I want.' One replied, 'Nay, but you want a hundred and fifteen pounds to pay for the lease of the Foundery, and likewise a large sum of money to put it into repair.' On this consideration I suffered them to subscribe. And when the society met I asked, 'Who will take the trouble of receiving this money, and paying it where it is needful?' One said, 'I will do it, and keep the account for you.' So here was the first steward. Afterward I desired one or two more to help me as stewards, and in process of time a greater number."

2. "The business of stewards," says Mr. Wesley, in his usual laconic style, "is,—

a. "To manage the temporal things of the society.

b. "To receive the subscriptions and contributions.

c. "To expend what is needful, from time to time.

d. "To send relief to the poor.

e. "To keep an exact account of all receipts and expenses.

f. "To inform the minister if any of the rules of the society are not punctually observed.

g. "To tell the preachers in love, if they think any thing amiss either in their doctrine or life.

"The rules of stewards are:

a. "Be frugal. Save every thing that can be saved honestly.

b. "Spend no more than you receive. Contract no debts.

c. "Have no long accounts. Pay every thing within the week, or as soon as possible.

d. "Give none that asks relief either an ill word or an ill look. Do not hurt if you cannot help them.

e. "Expect no thanks from man."— *Wesley's Works,* vol. v, p. 185.

The duties of stewards are numerous and responsible. They relate, in part, to the effective operations of the pastorate, and in part to the pecuniary arrangements of the circuit. Though stewards may have but little to do in determining the estimated amount to be raised, yet the amount which is actually paid for the support of the pastor depends almost exclusively upon their efforts. Stewards are ordinarily the types of the pecuniary character of the societies which they represent. Where energetic and effective stewards are employed, poverty will vie with wealth, and comparatively small and feeble societies will amply sustain the institutions of the Church.

Stewards should endeavor to induce all the members of the Church to contribute statedly to every benevolent enterprise, as a matter of religious principle. Spasmodic efforts to raise an unusual amount for any institution, or for some admired preacher, are always attended with disastrous reaction, and greatly embarrass all financial arrangements. The amount which is paid ought never to be graduated by the popularity of the preacher, but by the condition of the Church, and the ability with which God has blessed it.

Stewards should endeavor to raise the preacher's claim by quarterly installments. This plan can be executed in most places, and can be at least partially executed in all. The expenses of the preacher in moving upon the circuit should be paid to him on his arrival at his charge. This amount has actually been paid by the preacher in advance, in his efforts to serve them; and justice demands that actual expenditures for their benefit should immediately be met. Promptitude under such circumstances is appreciated far beyond the intrinsic value of the offering made: it furnishes an unmistakable welcome to the preacher, and a cordiality most gratifying to his heart.

Stewards should see that every subscription is collected when it becomes payable. It is of no avail to raise subscriptions unless prompt and systematic efforts are made for their collection.

Every regular attendant on the ministry of the word should be solicited, in a proper manner, to aid in the support of the Gospel. None will be offended who are approached with Christian courtesy; and the privileges which their own money helps to secure will be more highly prized by them.

The steward should remember that if he fail to discharge his duties, the cause of God will inevitably suffer. No other member of the Church feels at liberty to act in his capacity without appointment; and unless the finances of the Church are properly managed, the ministry must be embarrassed, or retire from their work.

3. The preacher in charge, previous to 1812, had the power to *appoint* stewards. Since that time he has possessed only the right of *nomination*—the power of appointment being vested in the quarterly conference.

4. Stewards hold their office for one year, but may be reappointed from year to year. They are responsible to the quarterly conference for the faithful discharge of their official duties; and the quarterly conference may dismiss or change them at pleasure, without preferring any formal charge.

5. Since the year 1820, one of the stewards has been specifically appointed a recording steward. This office, however, does not constitute him, *ex officio*, the secretary of the quarterly conference. His duties require him to record the doings of the quarterly conference, and the Sabbath-school quarterly reports. In other respects the prerogatives and duties of recording stewards are the same as those of other stewards.

6. A preacher in charge has no right to accept the resignation of a steward, and declare the office vacant. The quarterly conference, which confers the office, can alone accept of the resignation.

7. When two or more circuits or stations are united, the stewards shall hold office till the first quarterly conference shall elect a new board. (Gen. Conf. Jour., 1868.)

CHAPTER VIII.
RULES OF ORDER.

1.—*Parliamentary Rules.*

EVERY pastor will frequently be called to preside over the deliberations of others, and hence should be well versed in all that relates to the correct and orderly management of deliberative bodies.

The preacher in charge is the presiding officer in leaders' meetings, in the Sunday-school board, in the meetings of such boards of trustees as are appointed according to Discipline, in quarterly conferences, in the absence of the presiding elder, in the arbitration and trial of members, in the missionary committees, and in the committee of local preachers called to investigate the case of an accused local preacher.

2.—*Temporary Organization.*

It frequently happens that a temporary organization is necessary. In such cases, some person of age, or distinction, should rise and call the meeting to order, announcing the arrival of the time of the meeting, and suggesting an organization, by the appointment of a chairman before proceeding to business. The same person should act until a chairman is selected. Some four or five persons may be nominated as chairman. The question should not be put until every nomination that is desired is made. The names of the nominees should then be announced, in the order in which the nominations were made, and the question submitted to the assembly. When a majority of votes is given for any candidate, he should be declared president *pro tem.*, and invited to the chair, without voting upon the other names.

The president *pro tem.*, having taken the chair, should conduct the religious services of the occasion, or call upon some competent person to do so.

After prayer, a secretary *pro tem.* should be appointed. If several secretaries are appointed, the one first named is the principal officer.

In all deliberative representative assemblies it is necessary to ascertain who are properly members. This should be done, by general consent, either before or after the permanent organization, and before proceeding to any other business. This may be done by the secretary, who may receive the credentials and record the names of members, or by a committee appointed for this purpose.

In case the seat of a member is contested, he should be heard in his own defense, and then retire until the case is determined. The other members, who are legally appointed, form a court to determine the question of all contested elections, unless they refer it to a committee.

3.—*Permanent Organization.*

This is usually done in one of two ways. First, by raising a committee to nominate a full board of officers for the association, and proceeding to ballot, or to confirm the nomination by vote; or, secondly, by promiscuously nominating the different officers *viva voce*, and then balloting or confirming by hand-vote.

4.—*Presiding Officer.*

The duties of a presiding officer are the following:

To call the members to order at the appointed time.

To conduct the religious services.

To direct the roll to be called at the opening

of each session, unless otherwise ordered, and the records of the previous meeting to be read.

To announce the order of business, if any manifesto has been put forth respecting it.

To receive all messages and communications, and announce them to the meeting.

To put to vote all questions which are regularly submitted, or necessarily arise in the course of the proceedings, and declare the result.

To see that the laws of debate, and due order and decorum, are observed by the members.

To decide all questions of order.

To authenticate, by his signature, all the acts and proceedings of the assembly.

To appoint committees, when directed in a particular case, or when a standing rule requires it; and, in general, to obey implicitly its commands.

The chairman ought to give direct and serious attention to each individual while speaking, and to hold no conversation with any one at the time.

The utmost impartiality should be observed. Minorities and opponents should have their interests as jealously guarded as those of the majority, or of most intimate friends.

When the president withdraws from the chair, the vice-president should take his place. If there be no vice-president, custom allows the president to appoint a chairman during his temporary absence.

If, in the absence of the president, it becomes necessary to choose a president *pro tem.*, it is the duty of the secretary to conduct the proceedings.

In large assemblies, the presiding officer may *read sitting*, but should *rise* to state a motion or put a question.

5.—*Secretary.*

The general duties of the recording officer of a deliberative body are the following:

To keep a correct record of the proceedings of the assembly.

To read all papers which may be ordered to be read.

To notify the chairman of each committee of his appointment, giving him a list of his colleagues, and stating the business referred to them.

To authenticate, by his signature, all the acts of the assembly.

To preserve all the papers and documents of the assembly, and allow none to be taken from his table without a formal leave of the assembly.

The secretary, if a member of the body, is not

deprived of the privilege of taking part in the deliberations of the meeting.

The secretary should stand while reading or calling the roll of the assembly.

He should write a clear, legible hand; and all items of business, for the sake of easy reference, should be recorded in separate paragraphs.

The peculiar duties of the secretary of an annual conference are the following:

a. To aid the president in the organization of the conference by reading the roll of the members at the opening of each annual session. This is usually done by the secretary of the previous session.

b. To furnish the bishop with answers to questions 21st, 29th, 30th, and 31st of the business of conference, (Discipline, ¶ 78,) for the General Minutes.

c. To countersign all drafts upon the Book Concern and Chartered Fund.

d. To report annually to the secretaries of the Missionary Society the names of missions in the Conference, and the sum appropriated to each. (Discipline, ¶ 81.)

e. To report to the Sunday-School Union the number and condition of the Sunday-schools in the Conference. (Discipline, ¶ 85.)

The journals of the annual conferences are subject to the inspection of the General Conference, and should be executed in the best manner, as it regards penmanship, arrangement, and mode of reference. The heading of every page should give the date; and the margin, references to all the transactions recorded.

6.—*Members.*

All members have an equal right to submit propositions to the assembly, and to explain and recommend them in discussion.

No member should be interrupted when speaking, except by the president, to call him to order when he departs from the question, uses personalities or disrespectful language; but any member may call the attention of the president to the subject when he deems a speaker out of order: and any member may explain, if he thinks himself misrepresented.

A member who violates the rules of decorum may be *named* by the president; that is, the president may declare that such a member, calling him by name, is guilty of certain improper conduct. The member thus accused is entitled to be heard in his own defense, and must then withdraw.

The only punishments which a deliberative

body can inflict are reprimanding, prohibition to speak or vote for a specified time, and expulsion. It may require the offender to ask pardon, on pain of expulsion.

Any member who desires to speak must respectfully address the chair.

If two members address the president nearly at the same time, he should give the floor to the one whose voice he first heard. If the decision of the president is not satisfactory to any member, the opinion of the assembly may be taken on it.

7.—*Motions.*

When a motion has been made and seconded, the presiding officer must state it to the assembly before it is in their possession.

No speech should be made without a motion, nor after a motion is submitted, until it is seconded, and stated by the president.

All motions or resolutions, introduced by any member, must be reduced to writing, if the president, secretary, or any two members request it.

According to the rules of the House of Representatives, and those of the General Conference, any motion or resolution may be withdrawn by the mover, at any time, before decision or amendment.

No new motion or resolution can be made until the one under consideration is disposed of; which may be done by adoption or rejection, unless one of the following motions should intervene, which motions must have precedence in the order in which they are placed, namely, adjournment, indefinite postponement, laying on the table, reference to a committee, postponement to a given time, a substitute which may be amended, amendment.

All motions should be put in an affirmative and not in a negative form.

8.—*Indefinite Postponement.*

If a motion has been indefinitely postponed, it cannot be called up or resumed during that session. If a negative decision has been given, it has no effect whatever on the final disposal of the question.

9.—*Laying on the Table.*

This motion is proper when the assembly wishes for more information upon the subject. If decided in the affirmative, the principal motion, and all subsidiary questions connected with it, are removed from before the assembly until they are taken up again, which may be done at any time, at the pleasure of the assembly. If they are not taken up, it is equivalent to an indefinite postponement.

10.—*Referring to a Committee.*

When a proposition is regarded with favor and some modifications are desired, it is usual to refer it to a committee—to the standing committee, if one has been raised on that subject; otherwise, to a select committee.

If it is suggested to refer it both to a standing and to a select committee, the question should be first put in reference to the standing committee. A portion only of a subject may be referred, and different portions may be referred to different committees.

If a committee make a report, and the assembly wish for certain alterations or amendments, it may *recommit* the report.

If a subject is referred with instructions, those instructions, of course, must be obeyed.

11.—*Division of a Question.*

When a proposition consists of two or more parts, so independent and distinct that if one be taken away the others will remain entire, and it is supposed that the assembly may approve of some but not of all the parts, it is frequently more desirable to resolve it into its elementary parts than to attempt to modify it by amendments.

Where a deliberative body has adopted no rule providing for the division of complicated questions, no division should take place without a definite motion to divide, unless a unanimous consent is given.

12.—*Filling Blanks.*

When blanks are left for the assembly to fill, the proposition to fill is not an amendment, but an original motion.

In filling blanks where different numbers are named, the question should be put first on *the largest sum* and *the longest time.*

13.—*Amendments.*

The mover may modify or accept of an amendment when it is made, before it has been stated to the assembly by the chairman. In this case it becomes a part of the original motion. In all other cases it must be put as a regular amendment.

Rules respecting Amendments.—Amendments may be made in three ways: by striking out certain words, or by inserting certain words, or by striking out some and inserting other words.

1. When a proposition consists of several sen-

tences or resolutions, it should be taken up in order, and each paragraph amended according to the pleasure of the assembly : and when it is thus passed through, it is not deemed orderly to introduce new amendments into the first part of the proposition.

2. Every amendment may be amended; but it can go no further. There cannot be an amendment to an amendment of an amendment. The question should first be put on the last amendment, and proceed in that order.

3. Whatever is agreed to by the assembly, on a vote, either adopting or rejecting a proposed amendment, cannot afterward be altered or amended.

4. The converse of the above rule is true. Whatever is disagreed to by the assembly, on a vote, cannot afterward be moved again.

Striking out.—If an amendment to strike out is rejected, it cannot be moved again to strike out the same words, or a part of them; but it may be moved to strike out the same words, or a part of them, with other words. But if the amendment to strike out is agreed to, it cannot afterward be moved to insert the same words, or a part of them, unless it is proposed to insert other words in connection with them. The same rule applies in reference to inserting the same words, or a part of them. The motion to amend those relating to striking out and inserting applies as in other cases of amendment.

Striking out and inserting.—If the motion is divided, the question is first to be taken on sriking out; and if that is decided in the affirmative, then on inserting: but if the former is decided in the negative, the latter of course falls.

If the motion to strike out and insert is put undivided, and decided in the negative, the same motion cannot again be renewed. But it may be moved to strike out and,

1. Insert nothing; or,
2. Insert other words; or,
3. Insert the same, with other words; or,
4. Insert a part of the same words with others; or,
5. Strike out the same words with others, and insert the same; or,
6. Strike out a part of the same words with others, and insert the same; or,
7. Strike out other words, and insert the same; or,
8. Insert the same words without striking out any thing. (Ref. Cushing's Manual.)

On putting the question, first read the passage proposed to be amended as it stands, then the words proposed to be struck out or inserted; and, lastly, the whole passage as it will stand if the amendment be adopted.

Defeating a Proposition.—Amendments may be made to a proposition, which will not only modify the meaning, but convey a directly opposite sense; and often, in legislative bodies, bills are amended by striking out all after the enacting clause, and inserting a new bill; and resolutions are amended by striking out all after the words " resolved that," and inserting a proposition of an entirely different character.

14.—*Privileged Questions.*

Questions of this nature are of three kinds: 1. Motions to adjourn. 2. Motions relating to the rights and privileges of the assembly, or of its members individually. 3. Motions for the orders of the day.

15.—*Adjournment.*

A simple motion to adjourn cannot be amended, but must be decided without debate. A motion to adjourn to a particular day is debatable, and may be amended in regard to time.

"A motion to adjourn is not in order, 1. When a member is speaking; 2. When a vote is being taken on any question; 3. A motion to adjourn being negatived, cannot be renewed until some other proposition is made, or other business transacted."—*Matthias's Manual*, p. 72; *Cushing's Elements of Law and Practice*, p. 545.

An adjournment without day is equivalent to a dissolution.

When a question is interrupted by adjournment before any vote is taken upon it, it is thereby removed from the assembly, and does not stand before it at its next regular session, but must be brought forward in the usual way. But an adjourned special meeting is regarded as a continuation of a former meeting, and the business should be resumed the same as if no adjournment had taken place.

16.—*Orders of the Day.*

When the consideration of a subject has been assigned by the assembly to a certain day, it is called the order of the day.

If any other proposition arise on the day assigned for the consideration of any subject, a motion for the order of the day will supersede such proposition, and must be first put and decided.

To entitle this motion to precedence, it must be for the orders of the day generally, if there is more than one, and not for any particular subject; and the orders must be taken up in the order in which they stand.

If a subject is assigned for any particular hour, the question to proceed to it is not a privileged one until the hour has arrived; but if no hour is fixed, the order is for the entire day and every part of it.

If the motion for the orders of the day prevails, the original question is removed from the consideration of the assembly, in the same manner as if it had been interrupted by an adjournment. If the motion is decided in the negative, the orders of the day must be superseded until that subject is disposed of.

The orders of the day, unless disposed of on the day assigned, fall, and must be renewed for some other day.

17.—*Incidental Questions,*

Such as questions of order, motions for the reading of papers, leave to withdraw a motion, suspension of a rule, and amendment of an amendment, must be decided before the questions which gave rise to them.

18.—*Questions of Order.*

It is the duty of the presiding officer to enforce the rules of the assembly; and any member noticing a breach of the rule may call his attention to it, and insist upon the enforcement of it.

When a question of order arises, all other business must be suspended until that point is settled. The presiding officer must decide the point without debate. If the decision is not satisfactory, any member may appeal to the assembly. The question should then be stated: "Shall the decision of the chair stand as the decision of the assembly?" When it is thus stated it is debatable, and the presiding officer may participate in the debate. When a question has been put, and the decision announced, if any member alleges that the question was not understood, the presiding officer may recall his decision and put the question again.

19.—*Previous Question.*

The design of the previous question is chiefly for suppressing debate, and taking immediate action on the main question.

The question is put in this form: "Shall the main question be now put?" If it is decided in the negative, the debate continues; if in the affirmative, the vote must be at once taken, in the form in which the question exists at the time.

A previous question cannot be amended. By the rules of the House of Representatives, the previous question can only be admitted when demanded by a majority of the members present; and if it is ordered it brings the House to a direct vote upon a motion to commit, if such motion shall have been made; and if this motion does not prevail, then upon amendments reported by a committee, if any; then upon pending amendments, and then upon the main question. It is not in order to move the previous question unless the assembly has adopted the rule for its government. When the previous question is moved and seconded by the requisite number, all further amendments and discussion must cease. The president rises and says, "The previous question has been moved and seconded,—the question before the meeting is, 'Shall the main question be now put?'" If it is decided in the affirmative, the question should then be put, first on the amendments, and then on the main proposition.

20.—*Order of Proceeding.*

When the assembly does not prescribe any order of proceeding, the presiding officer may present any regular business according to his discretion. In an annual conference the regular disciplinary questions are presented by the bishop by disciplinary authority, and at his discretion as to time and circumstances.

In considering a proposition consisting of several paragraphs, the paper should first be read entirely through by the secretary, then a second time by the presiding officer or secretary, pausing at the close of every paragraph, that amendments may be made if desired ; and when the whole paper has been gone through with, in this order, the final question should be put on agreeing to, or adopting, the whole paper as amended or unamended.

When there is a preamble, it should be considered after the disposal of the resolutions or propositions under it. When a paper has been referred to a committee, and reported back with amendments, these amendments must first be disposed of, unless amended, before other amendments are introduced.

It is deemed an unparliamentary and abusive proceeding to introduce a proposition, and at the same time move the previous question. In such cases it is recommended by Judge Cushing to take no notice of the motion for the previous question.

21.—*Order in Debate.*

The presiding officer is not presumed to enter into the debate; but he is allowed to state matters of fact within his knowledge, to inform the assembly on points of order when called upon to do so, or when it is necessary to do so; and on appeals from his decision on questions of order, he may address the assembly in debate.

A member rising to address the assembly must respectfully address himself to the president, and not proceed until his name is called by that officer.

When two or more members rise at nearly the same time, the president must name the member who is first to speak. The person whose voice is first heard is entitled to the floor. If the assembly is not satisfied with the decision of the chair, the question should be put first in reference to the person named by the president; and if it is decided in the negative, then upon the name of the person for whom the floor is claimed in preference to him.

When a person gives way to another to speak, he really resigns the floor, and can retain it only by general consent, or the vote of the assembly.

When the presiding officer rises to speak, any

other member should be seated until he is first heard; but this does not authorize any presiding officer to interrupt a speaker unless he is out of order.

Every member should confine himself directly to the subject of debate; but the presiding officer should not generally interpose, unless the remarks are manifestly irrelevant.

When called to order for irrelevancy, the speaker may proceed, unless a motion prevail that he is out of order. And in this case, by usual parliamentary rules, he may proceed, if he abandons his objectionable course of remark; but by the Rules of the House of Representatives such speakers are not allowed to proceed, if any member objects, without leave of the House.

No member should speak more than once upon the same question without the permission of the assembly, unless it be to explain, although the debate on the question may be continued through several days.

Respectful attention should be paid to every speaker.

If a member uses offensive and abusive language toward other members, he may be stopped by one or more rising for that purpose, or by the president; and the words objected to should be written down by the secretary, that the offender may disclaim or apologize for the offense, or receive the censure of the assembly.

22.—*Taking the Question.*

A proposition made to a deliberative body is called a *motion;* when propounded to the assembly for reception or rejection, it is denominated a *question;* when adopted it becomes the *order, resolution,* or *vote* of the assembly.

Strictly speaking, no question can arise in a deliberative assembly without a motion being first made and seconded ; yet sometimes, for the dispatch of business, the presiding officer takes it for granted that a motion has been made, and puts the question accordingly.

The question being stated, the president puts it first in the affirmative : " As many as are of opinion that, [repeating the question,] say Aye," or " raise your hands;" and, putting it in the negative, " As many as are of a different opinion," etc.

If the presiding officer is doubtful as to the majority of voices, he may put the question a second time ; or, if he is still doubtful, or a member doubts the vote, he may direct the assembly to divide, and appoint tellers to return the several divisions of the house ; or the secretary to count the number who rise in voting.

Every person is bound, unless excused, to vote on every question.

A person not present when the vote is taken, cannot vote afterwards without permission of the assembly.

If the members are equally divided upon a question, the presiding officer ordinarily may give the casting vote. This rule, however, does not apply to the president of annual, of district, or of quarterly conferences.

If a question arises upon a point of order— for example, as to the right or the duty of a member to vote while a division is taking place—the presiding officer must decide it peremptorily, subject to the correction of the assembly after the division is over.

If a quorum is not present when a division takes place, there can be no decision.

23.—*Reconsideration.*

When any motion or resolution has been carried in the affirmative or negative, it is in order for any member who voted in the majority to move for a reconsideration of it.

The passage of a resolution to reconsider places the question where it was before decision, and leaves it open for discussion, amendment, adoption, or rejection.

24.—*Committees.*

Committees appointed to consider a particular subject are called *select committees;* those appointed to consider all subjects of a similar nature are denominated *standing committees.*

It is customary, in all deliberative bodies, to constitute a majority of the committee of such persons as are known to be favorably inclined to the measure proposed.

The person first named on a committee is the chairman to call the first meeting; but every committee may elect its own chairman to preside over its deliberations.

They may receive instructions when the business is at first referred to them, or at any subsequent period. A committee is not at liberty to sit while the assembly is sitting, without special permission. It can act only when regularly assembled together as a committee—a separate consultation and consent is not binding. If a paper has been referred to a committee, and it is entirely opposed to it, it ought not to suppress it, but report it back to the assembly with its objections. The paper should not be erased, interlined, or disfigured. If amendments are proposed to it, they should be written on a separate piece of paper. The report may be made to the assembly by the chairman, or by any other person who shall be authorized to do so.

25.—*Reports of Committees.*

Every report should be written fully and plainly, without erasure or interlinear lines, and signed either by the chairman and secretary, or by all the members of the committee.

A report may be received by direct vote, or the general consent of the assembly.

A report may consist merely of a statement of facts, reasoning, or opinion, or simply of a series of resolutions, or of both combined. When a report closes with a series of resolutions, the assembly should first act on the resolutions, and then on the preliminary remarks.

When the report of a select committee is accepted, the committee is discharged.

26.—*Minority Report.*

"Should a committee not be unanimous in opinion, and those in the minority be desirous of placing their views before the meeting, the matter should be introduced immediately after the majority report has been read. A member will then move that 'the report and resolution thereto attached be postponed for the present, for the purpose of enabling the minority to make a report as a substitute.' If this motion prevails, as is almost always the case, the minority report will be immediately presented, received, and read. It is then in order, on motion, to take up for consideration the resolution attached to either of the reports."—*B. Matthias's Manual*, p. 38.

Or when the majority report is considered, the minority report may be moved as an amendment, or a substitute for it.

A protest cannot be inserted on the journal without the consent of the majority.

27.—*Committee of the Whole.*

When a subject has been ordered to be referred to a Committee of the Whole, the mode of organizing such committee is as follows: A motion is made and seconded that the assembly do now resolve itself into a Committee of the Whole for the purpose of considering the matter relating to ——, naming the subject. If the question prevails, the president will call some member to the chair, or the assembly may appoint a chairman.

The committee, thus organized, is under the same laws that govern assemblies, with the following exceptions:

1. The previous question cannot be moved.

2. The presiding officer of the assembly has the same privilege to take a part in the debate that the other members have.

3. They cannot, like other committees, adjourn to some other time or place; but when they rise, if their business is unfinished, they can ask permission of the assembly to sit again.

4. They cannot refer any matter to a subcommittee.

5. Members are not restricted as to the times of speaking.

6. The yeas and nays cannot be called.

7. There is no appeal from the decision of the chair on points of order.

When the committee has finished the business referred to it, a member moves that the committee rise, and that the chairman, or some other member, report their proceedings to the assembly, which, being carried, the president resumes his seat. The chairman should then say: "The Committee of the Whole has had under consideration the matter relating to ——, and has instructed me to report that," etc. The president then presents the report for the action of the assembly. If its business is unfinished, and it is resolved to rise, report progress, and ask leave to sit again, the chairman says: "The Committee of the Whole has had under consideration the subject of ——; but not having had time to complete the same, has instructed me to report that it has made progress therein, and begs leave to sit again." The president thereupon puts the question on giving the committee leave to sit again. If leave is not granted, the committee is of course dissolved.

28.—*Rules of the General Conference in* 1884.

1. The conference shall meet at 9 o'clock A.M., and adjourn at 1 o'clock P.M.; but may alter the time of meeting and adjournment at its discretion.

2. The president shall take the chair precisely at the hour to which the conference stood adjourned, and cause the same to be opened by the reading of the Scriptures, singing, and prayer; and on the appearance of a quorum shall have the journal of the preceding session read and approved, and the business of the conference shall proceed in the following order, namely:

(1.) The roll of conferences shall be called in alphabetical order for the presentation of appeals, resolutions, and miscellaneous business.

(2.) Reports, first of the standing, and then of the select committees; *provided*, always, that each call severally shall have been completed before either preceding one shall be repeated.

3. The president shall decide all questions of order, subject to an appeal to the conference; but in case of such appeal the question shall be taken without debate, except that the appellant may make a simple statement of the grounds of his appeal.

4. The president shall appoint all committees unless otherwise specially ordered by the conference.

5. On assigning the floor to any member of the conference, the president shall distinctly announce the name of the member to whom it is assigned, and the annual conference he represents.

6. Resolutions shall be written and presented in duplicate by the mover, and also all motions, if the president, secretary, or any two members request it.

7. When a motion is made and seconded, or a resolution introduced and seconded, or a report presented and read by the secretary or stated by the president, it shall be deemed in possession of the conference; but any motion or resolution may be withdrawn by the mover, with the consent of the conference, at any time before amendment or decision.

8. The motions to lay on the table, to take from the table, and for the previous question, shall be taken without debate.

9. No new motion or resolution shall be entertained until the one under consideration has been disposed of, which may be done by adoption or rejection, unless one of the following motions should intervene, which shall have precedence in the order in which they are placed, namely:

(1.) To fix the time to which the conference shall adjourn;

(2.) To adjourn;

(3.) To take a recess;

(4.) To lay on the table;

(5.) For the previous question;

(6.) To postpone to a given time;

(7.) To refer;

(8.) Substitute;

(9.) Amendment;

(10.) To postpone indefinitely.

A motion to amend an amendment shall be in order, and a substitute for both amendments may be received, which substitute may be amended, and, if a substitute be accepted, it shall operate as an amendment to the original proposition.

10. When any member is about to speak in

debate, or to deliver any matter to the conference, he shall rise and respectfully address the president, but shall not proceed until recognized by him.

11. No member shall be interrupted when speaking, except by the president to call him to order when he departs from the question, or uses personalities or disrespectful language; but any member may call the attention of the president to the subject when he deems a speaker out of order, and any member may explain when he thinks himself misrepresented.

12. When a member desires to speak to a question of privilege, he shall briefly state the question; but it shall not be in order for him to proceed until the president shall have decided it a privileged question.

13. No person shall speak more than twice on the same question, nor more than ten minutes at one time, without leave of the conference; nor shall any person speak more than once until every member choosing to speak shall have spoken. *Provided*, however, that a committee making a report shall in all cases be entitled to ten minutes to close the debate, either to oppose the motion to lay the report on the table, or, this permission not having been used, to close the debate on the motion to adopt. The com-

mittee shall not be deprived of its right to close the debate, even after the previous question has been ordered.

14. When any motion or resolution shall have been acted upon by the conference, it shall be in order for any member who voted with the prevailing side to move a reconsideration ; but a motion to reconsider a non-debatable motion shall be decided without debate.

15. No member shall absent himself from the service of the conference without leave, unless he is sick or unable to attend.

16. No member shall be allowed to vote on any question who is not within the bar at the time when such question shall be put by the president, except by leave of the conference when such member has been necessarily absent.

17. Every member who is within the bar at the time a question is put shall give his vote, unless the conference, for special reasons, shall excuse him.

18. No resolution altering or rescinding any rule of Discipline shall be adopted until it shall have been in the possession of the conference at least one day, and shall have been printed in the Daily Advocate.

19. It shall be in order for any member to call for the yeas and nays on any question be-

fore the conference; and if the call be sustained by one hundred members present, the vote thereon shall be taken by yeas and nays. If not so sustained, members voting in the minority, if the number voting in said minority is less than one hundred, may have their votes recorded by name.

20. It shall be in order to move that the question be taken without further debate on any measure pending, except in cases in which character is involved; and if sustained by a vote of *two thirds,* the question shall be taken.

21. The motion to adjourn shall be taken without debate, and shall always be in order, except, (1) when a member has the floor; (2) when a question is actually put, or a vote is being taken; (3) when the question is pending on seconding the demand for the previous question; (4) when the previous question has been called and sustained, and is still pending; and (5) when a motion to adjourn has been negatived and no business or debate has intervened.

22. Members presenting memorials, petitions, and other papers for reference, shall prepare the paper by writing in a plain hand on the back of it the following items, in the following order, namely:

(1.) Name of the member presenting the paper.

(2.) Conference from which it comes.

(3.) Pastoral charge of the conference sending it.

(4.) Subject to which it relates.

(5.) First name on the petition.

(6.) Number of other petitioners.

(7.) The Committee to which he desires it referred.

Papers thus presented shall be delivered to the secretary of the conference, and by him sent to the committee, according to indorsement, and announced in the journal of the day.

23. When any member shall move the reference of any portion of the journal of an annual conference to any committee, he shall at the same time furnish a copy of the portion he wishes referred, prepared as already provided in the case of memorials.

24. All resolutions contemplating verbal alterations of the Discipline shall state the language of the paragraph and the line proposed to be altered, and also the language proposed to be substituted.

25. All committees proposing changes of Discipline shall not only recite the paragraph and

line proposed to be amended, but also the paragraph, as amended, complete.

26. All written motions, reports, and communications to the conference shall be passed to the secretary, to be by him read to the conference.

27. All committees shall furnish duplicates of their reports.

28. A call for a vote by orders shall be made and seconded by members of the same order.

29. When voting by orders the separation shall be merely in regard to the taking, announcing, deciding, and recording the vote of each order on the question on which the separate vote is "demanded." Any incidental matter bearing upon such vote shall be decided by the conference acting "as one body." In taking the vote by orders, the names of the delegates, first of the ministerial and then of the lay delegates, shall be called, and each member shall answer aye or no.

30. All demonstrations of approval or disapproval during the progress of debate shall be deemed a breach of order.

31. These rules shall not be suspended, except by a vote of two thirds of the members present and voting.—*Journal*, 1884, p. 49.

Appeals of Traveling Ministers or Preachers.

"In all cases of trial and conviction under the provisions of ¶¶ 214–222, an appeal shall be allowed to a judicial conference, constituted as hereinafter provided, if the condemned person signify his intention to appeal at the time of his conviction, or at any time thereafter when he is informed thereof.

"The several annual conferences in the United States shall, at each session, select seven elders, men of experience and of sound judgment in the affairs of the Church, who shall be known as Triers of Appeals.

"When notice of appeal is given to the president of an annual conference, he shall proceed, with due regard to the wishes and rights of the appellant, to designate three conferences, conveniently near that from which the appeal is taken, whose Triers of Appeals shall constitute a judicial conference, and to fix the time and place of its session, and to give notice thereof to all concerned. When said conference shall have assembled it shall be competent to try appeals from any conference conveniently near, which may be presented to it, due notice having been given to all concerned.

"The appellant shall have the right of peremptory challenge, yet so that the triers present, and ready to proceed with the hearing, shall not fall below thirteen, which number shall be required for a quorum.

" A bishop shall preside in the judicial conference, and shall decide all questions of law, subject to an appeal to the General Conference. The conference shall appoint a secretary, who shall keep a faithful record of all the proceedings, and shall, at the close of the trial, transmit the records made and the papers submitted in the case, or certified copies thereof, to the secretary of the preceding General Conference, to be filed and preserved with the papers of that body. But if the case be remanded for a new trial, the papers submitted shall be returned to the secretary of the annual conference of which the accused is a member. And when the case of any preacher who has been suspended or expelled is remanded for a new trial, he shall be suspended from all ministerial service until the next ensuing session of the annual conference.

" It shall be the duty of the secretary of the annual conference carefully to preserve the minutes of the trial, whether before a committee or before the conference, and all the documents relating to the case, together with the charge or charges and the specification or specifications, which minutes and documents only, in case of an appeal from the decision of an annual conference, shall be presented to the judicial conference in evidence on the case.

"In all cases where an appeal is made, and admitted by the judicial conference, the appellant shall state, either personally or by his representative, the grounds of his appeal, showing cause why he appeals, and he shall be allowed to make his appeal without interruption. After which the representatives of the annual conference from whose decision the appeal is made shall be permitted to respond in presence of the appellant, who shall have the privilege of replying to such representatives, which reply shall close the pleadings on both sides. Counsel on both sides shall be members of an annual conference. This done, the parties shall withdraw, and the judicial conference shall decide the case.

"The General Conference shall carefully review the decisions of questions of law contained in the records and documents transmitted to it from the judicial conferences, and in case of serious error therein shall take such action as justice may require.

"Appeals from an annual conference in the United States not easily accessible may, at the discretion of the president thereof, be heard by a judicial conference selected from among the more central conferences. Appeals from a conference other than those in the United States may be heard by a judicial conference called to meet at or near New York by the bishop in charge of said conference; or the appeal may be heard directly by the General Conference.

"After a preacher shall have been regularly tried and expelled he shall have no privileges of society or sacraments in our Church without confession, contrition, and satisfactory reformation."—*Discipline*, 1884, ¶¶ 247-256.

CHAPTER IX.

FORMULAS.

Section I.—*Formulas for Preachers in Charge.*

WE would not attempt to settle the precise form in any given case, or intimate that other modes of expression may not be equally proper; but we submit the following brief forms, as general guides to young and inexperienced pastors:—

I.—CERTIFICATE OF CHURCH MEMBERSHIP.

This certifies that A. B., the bearer, is an acceptable member of the —— Methodist Episcopal Church in ——, and is affectionately commended to the fellowship of the Methodist Episcopal Church in ——, or in any other Church to which he may present this certificate. When admitted to another charge, his relation to this charge will cease.

——, 18   C. D., *Preacher in Charge.*

II.—EXHORTER'S LICENSE.

This may certify that A. B., the bearer, having been duly recommended by the class of which he is a member, is hereby authorized to hold meetings for prayer and exhortation in the Methodist Episcopal Church on N—— Circuit.

     C. D., *Preacher in Charge.*

——, N. Y.
—— Conference.
Jan. 1, 18 .

In case of renewal, let it be signed by the presiding elder, or by the preacher in charge, as president of the Quarterly Conference, "by the approval of the Quarterly Conference."

III.—NOTE OF RECOMMENDATION TO A LOCAL PREACHER.

This may certify that A. B., the bearer, is a regularly authorized Local Preacher (Elder or Deacon) in the Methodist Episcopal Church in D——, N—— Conference. A. B., *P. E. on E. Dis., N. Con.,* or
    C. D., *Pr. in Charge of D. Station.*

Jan. 1, 18 .
D——, N. H.

IV.—CLASS-BOOK.

Class-Book, No. 1. D—— Circuit, N. Conference. C. D., *Leader.* T. V., *Pr. in Charge.* Remember the fast on the Friday preceding each quarterly meeting. Jan. 1, 18 .	State in Life.	State in the Church.	MEMBERS.	Residence.	January. 1.	January. 9.	January. 15.	Collections.
	M.	F.	C. D., Leader.	P. st., 17	p.	p.	p.	$10 00
	M.	F.	A. B	D. st. 5.	p.	a.	p.	10 00
	M.	F.	E. F	K	a.	p.	p.	15 00
	W.	F.	G. H	S	p.	d.	p.	10 00
	Wd.	F.	J. K	M	p.	p.	s.	1 00
	S.	T.	L. M	P	p.	p.	p.	20 00
	S.	T.	N. P	Q	p.	p.	d.	5 00
	S.	T.	R. S	R	p.	a.	p.	0 50

Abbreviations.

M.—Married.
S.—Unmarried.
W.—Widower.
Wd.—Widow.
F.—Full connexion.
T.—On trial.
p.—Present.
a.—Absent.
s.—Sick.
d.—Out of town.

V.—CHURCH REGISTER FOR A SUCCESSOR.

This should contain the names and residences of the local preachers, stewards, class-leaders, and exhorters; the board of trustees, superintendents of Sabbath schools, and the members of the several classes; and also the general plan of the circuit, the time and place for Sabbath preaching, weekly lectures, and class and prayer-meetings.

VI.—REGISTER OF THE CHILDREN, TO BE LEFT FOR A SUCCESSOR.

Names.	Parents.	Residences.	Remarks.
A. D.	O. B.	10 Laurel-st.	
E. F.	K. L.	5 Orange-st.	
G. H.	M. N.	6 Elm-st.	

Sec. I.] FOR PREACHERS IN CHARGE.

VII.—Money for benevolent objects should be carefully done up in separate parcels, and distinctly labelled, as follows:—

$100.

MISSIONARY MONEY.

NEWLAND CIRCUIT.

C. D., *Pr. in Charge.*

$100.

AMER. BIBLE SOCIETY.

NEWLAND CIRCUIT.

C. D., *Pr. in Charge.*

VIII.—STEWARD'S CERTIFICATE.

This may certify that the estimate for the support of Rev. A. B., Preacher in Charge of Newland Circuit, for the conference year ending May 1, 18 , was $500. Whole claim paid.

C. R., ⎫
B. R., ⎬ *Stewards.*
P. S., ⎪
K. R., ⎭

IX.—BENEVOLENT INSTITUTIONS.

MEMBERSHIP.

Societies.	Annual Membership.	Life Membership.	Director for Life.	Manager for Life.	Patron for Life.
American Bible Society.	$3	$30*	$150	...	...
Missionary Society of the M. E. Church.........	2	20*	...	$150*	$500
Sunday-School Union of the M. E. Church.....	1	10*	50	...	...
Tract Society of the M. E. Church...............	1	10*	25	.	...

* At one time.

X.—WILLS.

As ministers are frequently called upon to write or advise in reference to the making of wills, we subjoin the following:—

I.—*Commencement of Wills.*

In the name of God. Amen.

I, (A. B., of C———, &c.,) being of sound mind and memory, do make, publish, and declare this my last will and testament.

II.—*Bequests and Devises.*

Let these be arranged in order, thus: "First. I give and bequeath unto —— the sum of —— dollars, and the receipt of the treasurer of the Society shall be a sufficient discharge therefor to my executors;" or, "I give and devise the following (here describe the property) to the trustees of ——, and its use to be controlled by the said trustees, or their successors in office, for the use and benefit of ——." (Here state the benevolent object to which it shall be applied.)

III.—*Appointment of Executor and in testimonium*

And I do hereby appoint C. D., of W——, to be the sole executor of this my last will and testament, hereby revoking, annulling, and declaring void all former wills by me at any time heretofore made.

In witness whereof I have hereunto set my hand and seal this —— day of ——, &c.

IV.—*Attestation of Wills.*

Signed, sealed, and declared by the said A. B. to be his last will and testament in the presence of us, who, at his request, and in his presence, and in the presence of each other have hereunto subscribed our names and respective places of residence as witnesses.

M. M., of C——, }
P. M., of C——, } A. B. { L. S. }
M. N., of C——. }

(Let there be three witnesses.)

If the will be signed by a third person for the testator, the attestation should be as follows:—

Signed by the said E. F. in our presence, and in the presence of the said A. B., and by his express direction, and by the said A. B. at the same time, published and declared as his last will and testament in the presence of the said E. F. and of us, who each, in the presence of the other and of the said A. B., and of the said E. F., have hereunto set our hands as subscribing witnesses.

254 FORMULAS. [Chap. IX.

SECTION II.—*Formulas for Presiding Elders.*

[In all cases of licensing a Local Preacher, or recommendation for admission to the traveling connection or for ordination by a *District Conference*, the license or recommendation should state that the person was duly recommended to the District Conference by the Society of which he is a member, or by the Quarterly Conference, as the case may be.]

I.—LICENSE OF A LOCAL PREACHER.

To all whom it may concern.

This may certify that A. B., the bearer, having been duly recommended by the society of which he is a member, and having been examined by us concerning his gifts, grace, and usefulness, is judged by us to be a proper person to be licensed, and is hereby authorized to preach the Gospel in the M. E. Church.

Done at a Quarterly Conference held at Newland, this second day of May, A. D. one thousand eight hundred and

Signed by order and in behalf of said conference.

N. M., *Secretary.*   C. P., *Presiding Elder.*

II.—RECOMMENDATION TO THE TRAVELLING CONNEXION.

To the Bishop and members of the N. Conference, to be held at L——, May 1, 18 .

DEAR FATHERS AND BRETHREN,—

We, the members of the Quarterly Conference of Newland Circuit, being acquainted with the gifts, grace, and usefulness of our brother N. P., do hereby recommend him as a suitable person to be admitted on trial in the travelling connexion, he having been examined by us on the subject of doctrines and discipline.

Done at a Quarterly Conference held at Newland, April 1, 18 , and signed by order and in behalf of said conference.

N. F., *Secretary.*   D. G., *Presiding Elder.*

III.—RECOMMENDATION FOR DEACON OR ELDER'S ORDERS.

> To the Bishop and members of the N. Conference, to be held at G——, May 1, 18 .
>
> DEAR FATHERS AND BRETHREN,—
> We, the members of the Quarterly Conference of Newland Circuit, being acquainted with the gifts, grace, and usefulness of our brother N. P., do hereby recommend him as a suitable person to be ordained deacon (or elder) in the Methodist Episcopal Church, he having been for four consecutive years a regularly licensed local preacher, (or having held the office of deacon for four consecutive years,) and having been examined before us on the subject of doctrines and discipline.
>
> Done at a Quarterly Conference held at Newland, Jan. 1, 18 , and signed in behalf of said Quarterly Conference.   P. G., *Presiding Elder.*
> S. H., *Secretary.*

If the local deacon cannot attend the annual conference, he must subscribe his name to a note like the following, which should be appended to the preceding recommendation:—

> This may certify that I firmly believe the doctrines taught by the Methodist Episcopal Church, and cordially approve of her form of Discipline.
> Newland, Jan. 1, 18 .   N. P.

It is recommended that in all cases the signature of the local deacon be appended to a note like the above, whether he can or cannot attend the annual conference.

www.ingramcontent.com/pod-product-compliance
Lightning Source LLC
Chambersburg PA
CBHW021357230426
43666CB00006B/552